LET'S GO 2
GRAMMAR and LISTENING
Activity Book

Susan Rivers

Oxford University Press

Review

Listen and match. 🎧

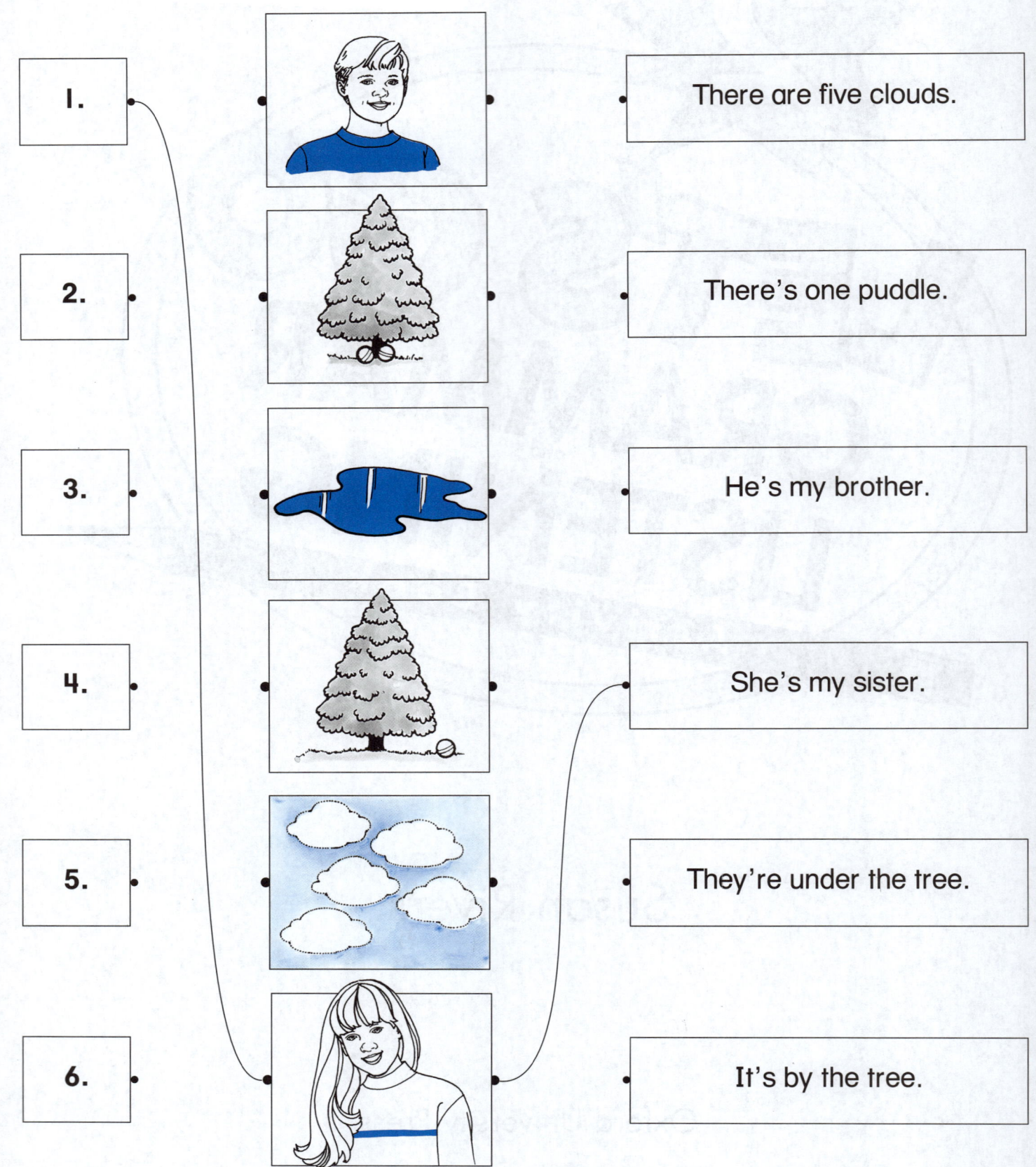

1.
2.
3.
4.
5.
6.

There are five clouds.

There's one puddle.

He's my brother.

She's my sister.

They're under the tree.

It's by the tree.

2

Listen, circle, and write. 🎧

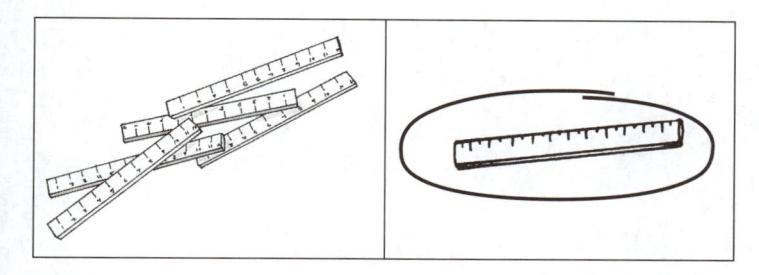

__b__ 1. a. They're rulers.
      b. It's a ruler.

____ 2. a. Yellow and black.
      b. Yellow and brown.

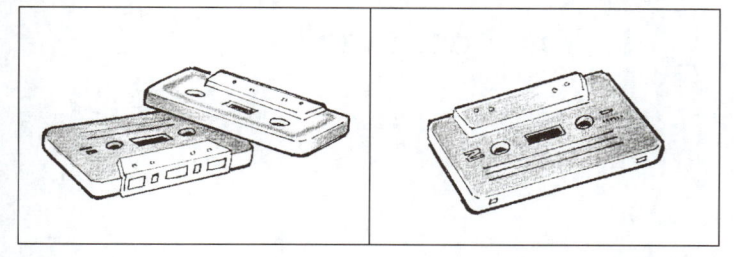

____ 3. a. Yes, they are.
      b. Yes, it is.

____ 4. a. Eight cassettes.
      b. Nine cassettes.

____ 5. a. It's a robot.
      b. It's a yo-yo.

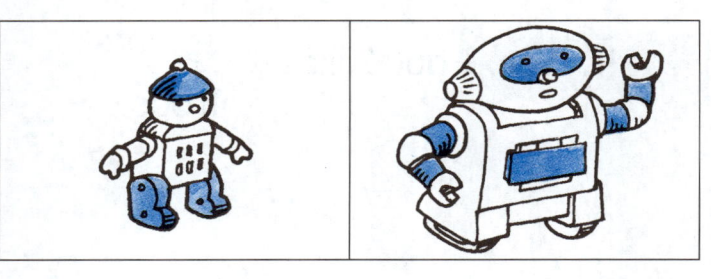

____ 6. a. It's a little robot.
      b. It's a big robot.

Review

A Listen and write a ✓ or an ✗.

__✗__ 1. I want fish.

_____ 2. I like rabbits.

_____ 3. I want milk.

_____ 4. I like birds.

B Listen and circle.

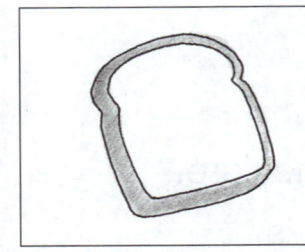

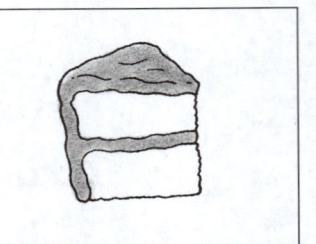

1. Yes, I do. I want   bread.
   (cake.)

2. No, I don't. I like   dogs.
   cats.

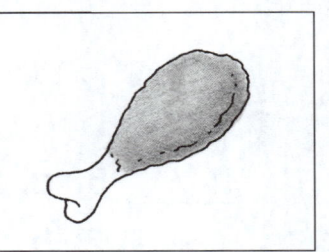

3. No, I don't. I want   pizza.
   chicken.

4. Yes, I do. I like   spiders.
   frogs.

Listen, look, and write. 🎧

| 1. g | 2. | 3. | 4. | 5. | 6. | 7. | 8. |

a. It's sunny.

b. Hello, Sarah.

c. I'm ten years old.

d. I like blue.

e. I'm fine. Thank you.

f. It's nice to meet you, too.

g. My name is Kate.

h. You're welcome.

Review

A. Listen, look, and match.

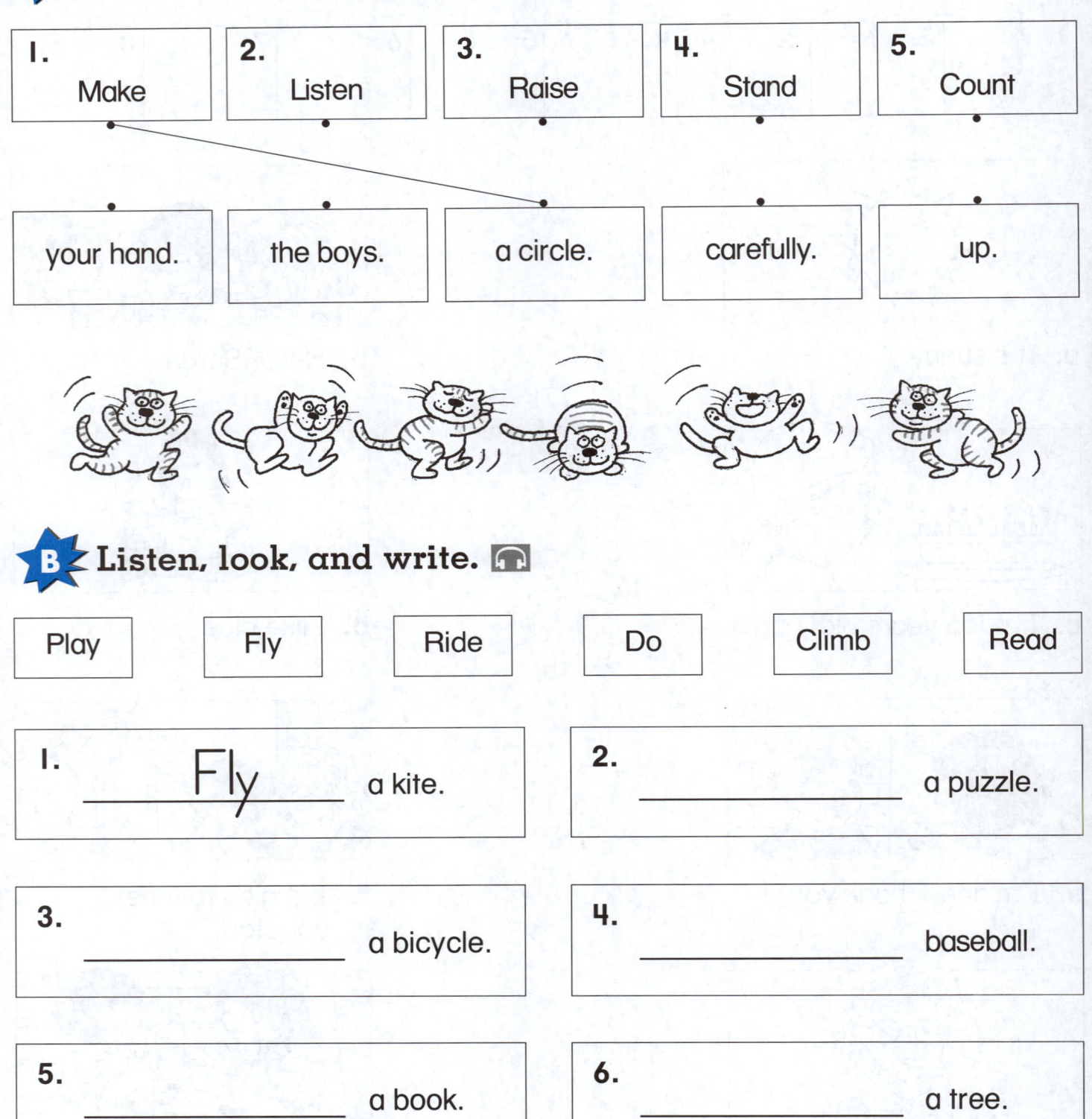

1. Make	2. Listen	3. Raise	4. Stand	5. Count
your hand.	the boys.	a circle.	carefully.	up.

B. Listen, look, and write.

| Play | Fly | Ride | Do | Climb | Read |

1. __Fly__ a kite.

2. _____ a puzzle.

3. _____ a bicycle.

4. _____ baseball.

5. _____ a book.

6. _____ a tree.

6

Listen, look, and write. 🎧

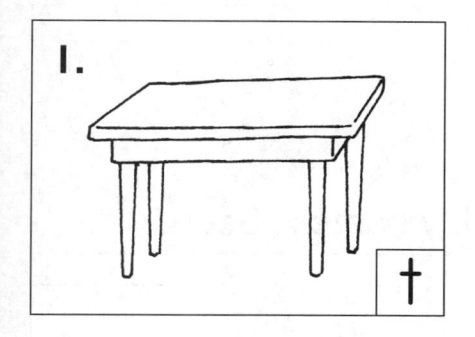

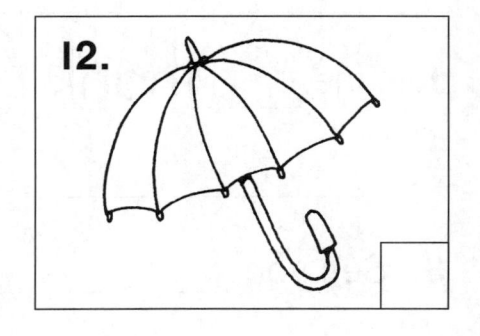

1. [table] t
2. [cat]
3. [egg]
4. [woman]
5. [octopus]
6. [fish]
7. [apple]
8. [van]
9. [desk]
10. [lion]
11. [girl]
12. [umbrella]

Unit 1

A Look and match.

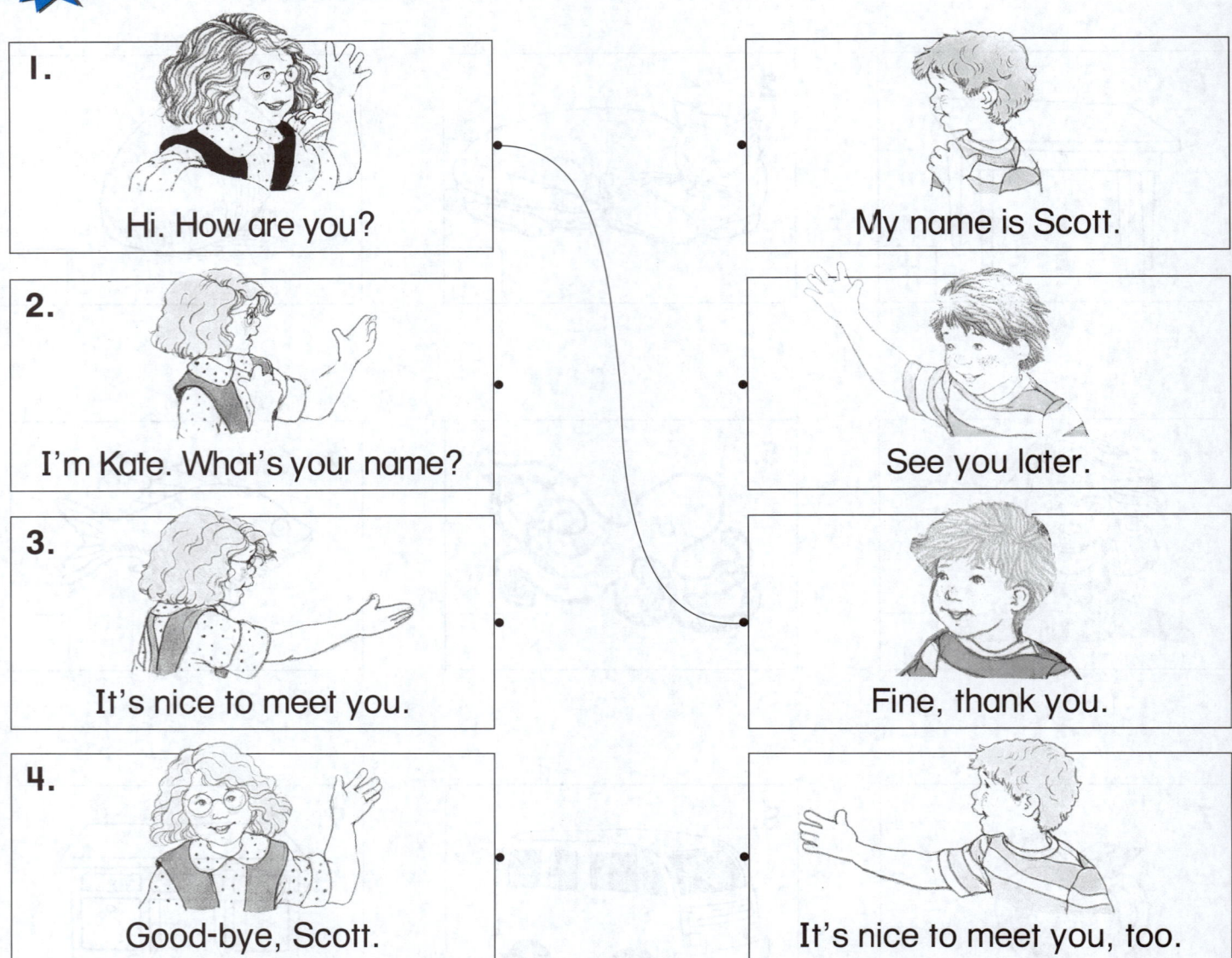

1. Hi. How are you?	My name is Scott.
2. I'm Kate. What's your name?	See you later.
3. It's nice to meet you.	Fine, thank you.
4. Good-bye, Scott.	It's nice to meet you, too.

B Choose and write.

| Good-bye | later | thank |

1. Fine, __thank__ you.

2. _____, Scott.

3. See you _____.

8

A. Unscramble the sentences.

1. you / are / How / ?

   How are you?

2. Fine, / you / thank / .

3. Scott / Good-bye, / .

4. See / later / you / .

B. Solve the puzzle.

1	2	3	4	5	6	7	8	9	10	11	12
a	s	l	o	y	r	t	e	g	u	z	i

S _ _   _ _ _   _ _ _ _ _ ,
2 8 8   5 4 10 3 1 7 8 6

_ _ _ _ _ _ _ _ _ !
1 3 3 12 9 1 7 4 6

9

A. Look and write.

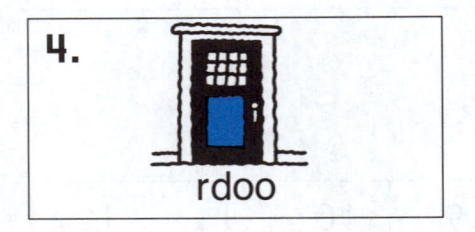

1. iwwdno — a __window__
2. okob — a _____
3. bealt — a _____
4. rdoo — a _____
5. sdke — a _____
6. hrcia — a _____

B. Look, read, and write.

1. 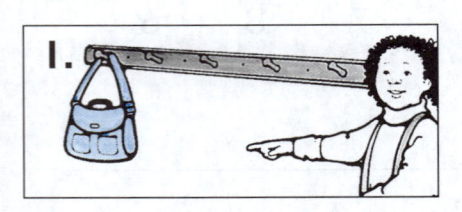 What is __that__? (this, (that))
   It is a __bag__.

2.  What is _____? (this, that)
   It is a _____ _____.

3.  What is _____? (this, that)
   It is a _____.

4.  What is _____? (this, that)
   It is a _____.

A. Look and write.

1. Is this a ruler? — Yes, it is.
2. Is that a notebook? — ___, ___ isn't.
3. Is this a ruler? — ___, ___ ___. 
4. Is that a bag? — ___, ___ ___.

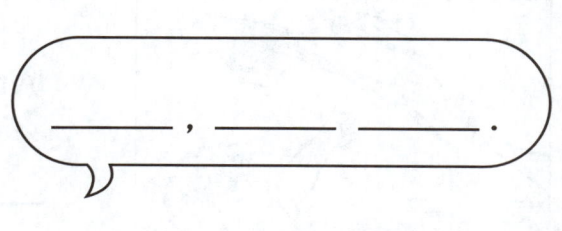

B. Read and write.

1. Is that a ruler?
   No, it isn't. It's a pen.

2. _____ 
   No, it isn't. It's an eraser.

3. _____ 
   Yes, it is. It's a crayon.

A Look and write.

1.  It's a yo-yo.
2.  They're kites.
3.  _____
4. _____

B Look, read, and write.

1.  What are ____those____ ? (these, (those))
   They're kites.

2.  What are _____ ? (these, those)
   _____

3.  What are _____ ? (these, those)
   _____

A. Look, read, and write.

1. Are those flowers?
Yes, they are.

2. Are these dogs?

3. Are those clouds?

B. Read, choose, and write.

a. Are those birds?
b. Are these frogs?
c. Are those dogs?
d. Are these trees?

b 1. Are these frogs?
No, they aren't. They're spiders.

___ 2.
Yes, they are. They're trees.

___ 3.
No, they aren't. They're cats.

___ 4.
Yes, they are. They're birds.

13

A. Listen and circle.

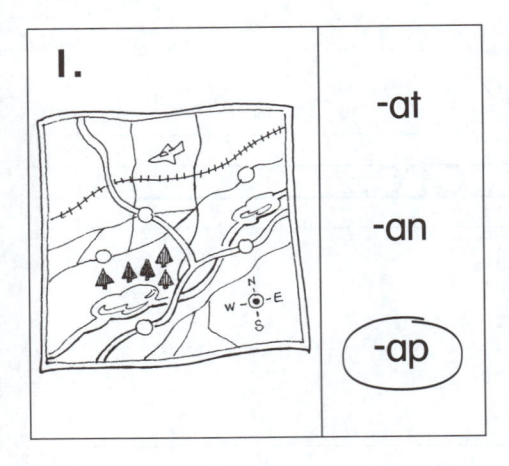

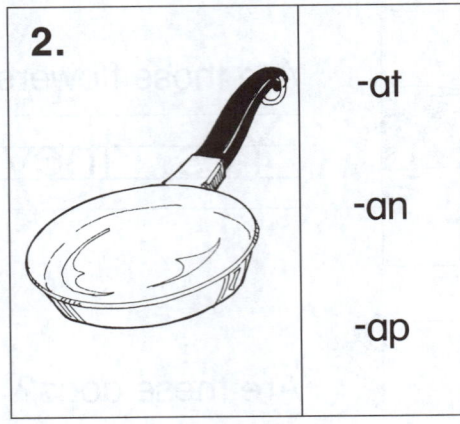

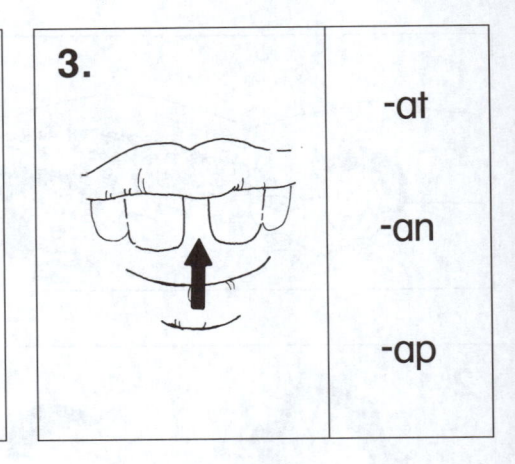

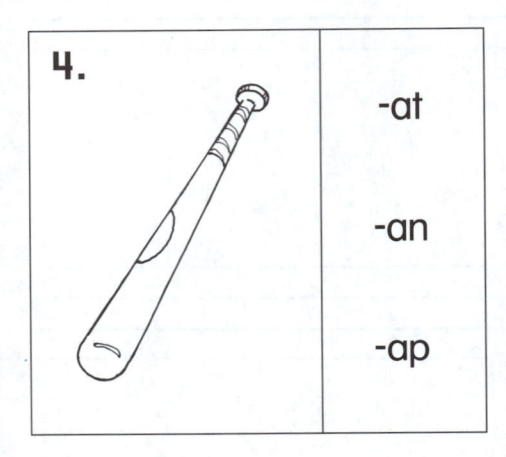

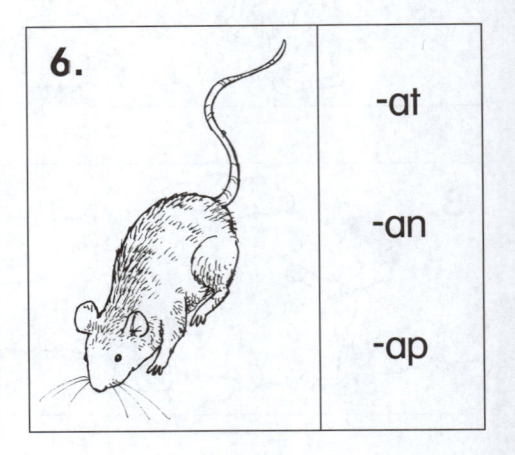

1. -at / -an / (-ap)
2. -at / -an / -ap
3. -at / -an / -ap
4. -at / -an / -ap
5. -at / -an / -ap
6. -at / -an / -ap

B. Listen and write *at*, *an*, or *ap*.

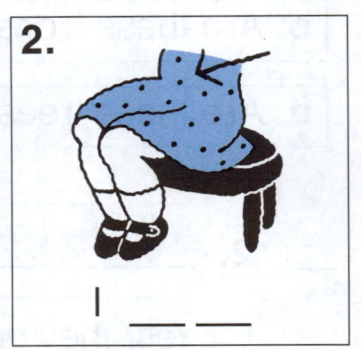

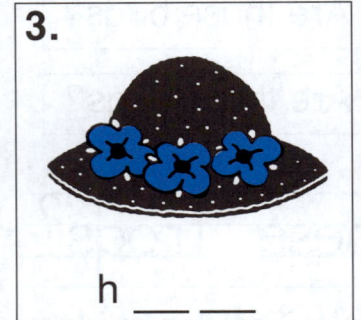

1. f a n
2. l __ __
3. h __ __
4. c __ __

C. Listen and write.

The c __ __ and the m __ __ are in the v __ __ .

14

A Listen and circle.

1.
   a. This is a door.
   b. (That's a door.)

2.
   a. This is a window.
   b. These are windows.

3.
   a. These are bicycles.
   b. Those are bicycles.

4.
   a. It's a crayon.
   b. They're crayons.

5.
   a. It's a spider.
   b. They're spiders.

6.
   a. No, it isn't.
   b. No, they aren't.

B Listen and write the letter.

1.	e
2.	
3.	
4.	
5.	
6.	

a. It's a puzzle.

b. Yes, they're trees.

c. They're puzzles.

d. These are trees.

e. That's a puzzle.

f. This is a tree.

15

Unit 2

A Read and write.

1. b
2. ___
3. ___
4. ___

a. Thanks.

b. Hi, John! What's the matter?

c. That's too bad. Get better soon.

d. I'm sick.

B Read and write.

1. What is = __What's__

2. That is = _____

3. I am = _____

A Look and write.

| 1. | 2. | 3. | 4. | 5. |

What's the matter?

1. I am sick.
2.
3.
4.
5.

B Read, choose, and write.

| too | matter | very | the | bad | today | sick |

1. What's the matter?
2. I am _____
3. That's _____

17

A Look and write.

1. nurse

B Look and write.

1. Mrs. Lee — Who's she?
She's Mrs. Lee.
She's a teacher.

2. Mr. White — Who's he?

3. Rita — Who's she?

18

A Answer the questions.

1. Is she a teacher?
No, she isn't.

2. Is he a farmer?

3. Is she a student?

4. Is he a taxi driver?

B Look, choose, and write.

| police officer | student | farmer |

1. Is she a ___police officer___?
No, she ___isn't___.

2. Is he a _____?
No, he _____.

3. Is she a _____?
Yes, she _____.

19

A. Look and write.

1.  He's <u>a student.</u>   They're students.
2.  She's _____   _____ 
3.  He's _____   _____

B. Look, read, and write.

Who are they?

1.  (Jones) They're Mr. and Mrs. Jones. They're farmers.
2.  (Long) _____
3. (Hill) _____

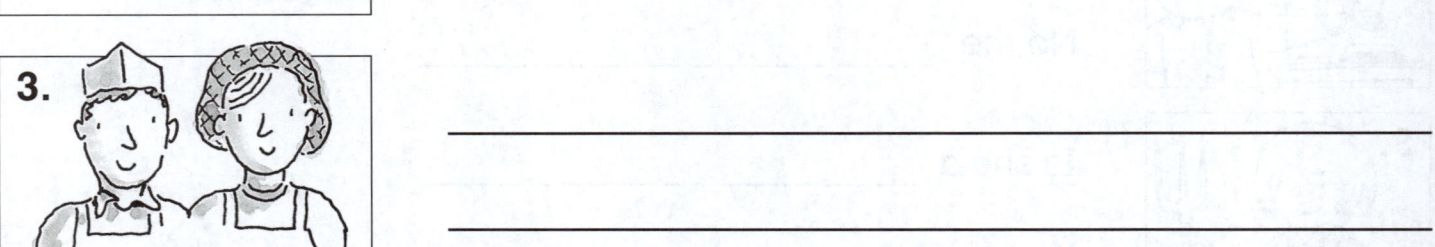

Match and answer the questions.

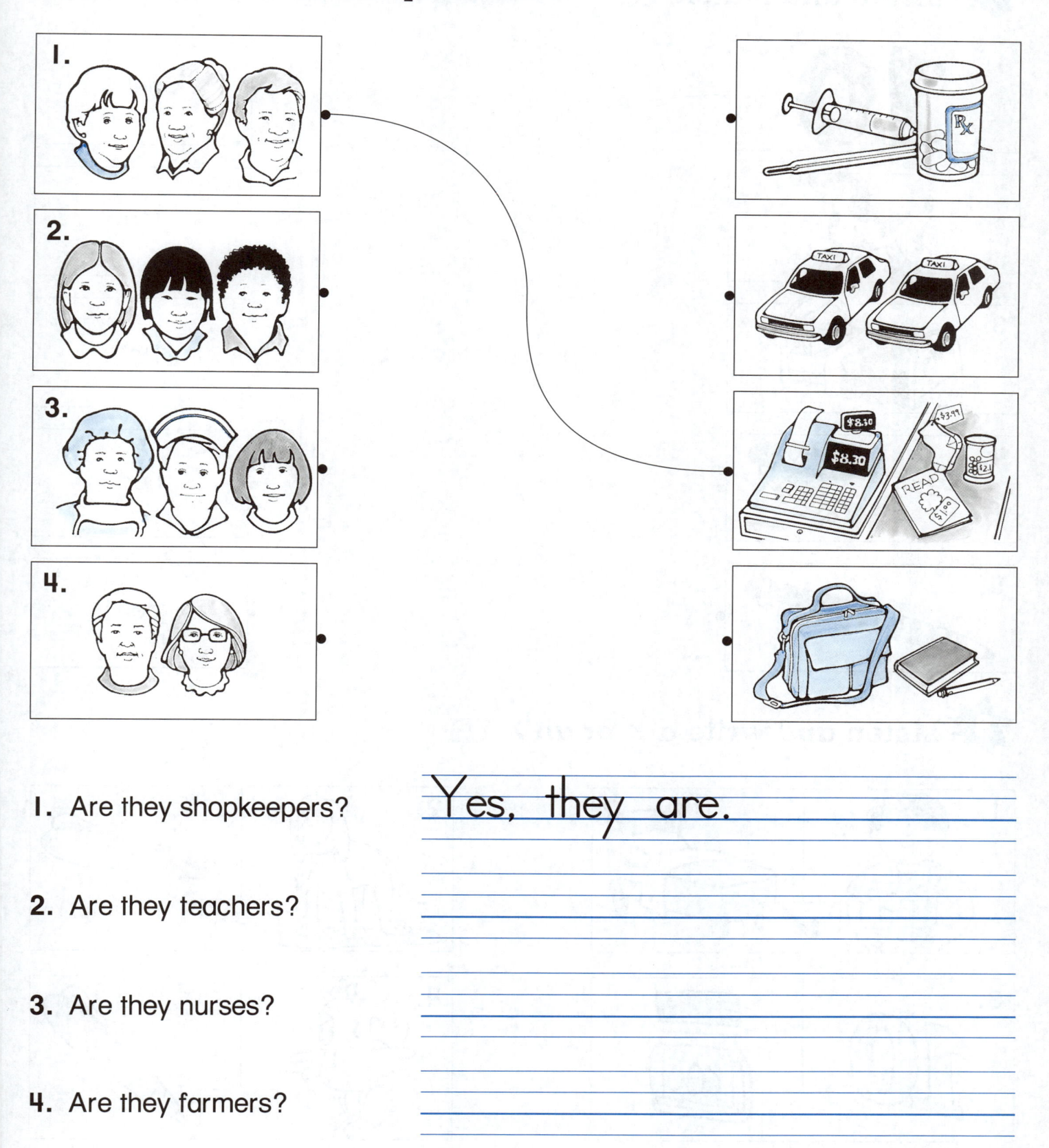

1. Are they shopkeepers?   Yes, they are.

2. Are they teachers?

3. Are they nurses?

4. Are they farmers?

21

A Listen and match.

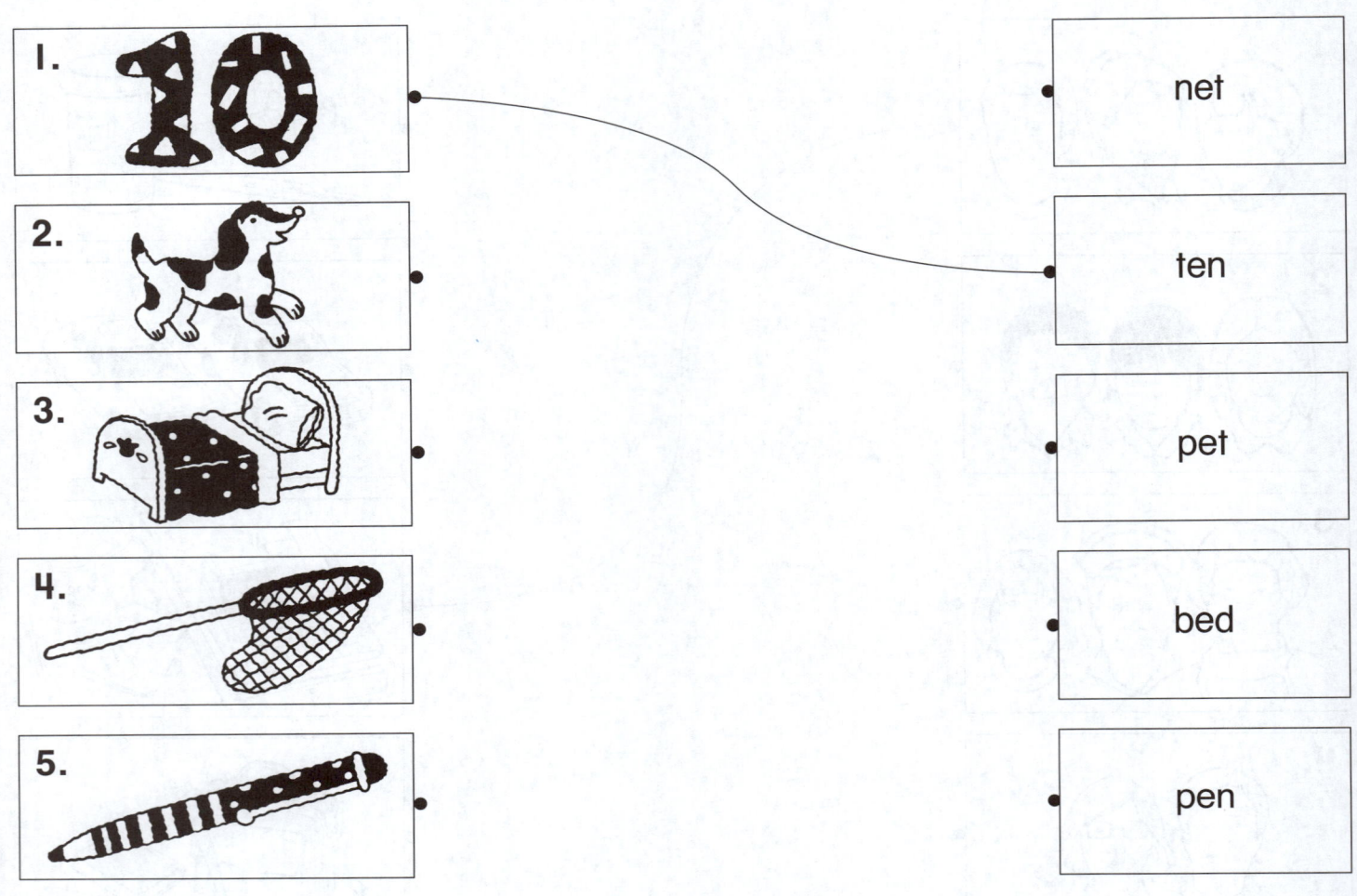

1. 10
2. (dog)
3. (bed)
4. (net)
5. (pen)

- net
- ten
- pet
- bed
- pen

B Listen and write a ✓ or an ✗.

1. Ted / bed — ✓
2. dog / pen
3. 10 / red
4. (chicken) / pen

22

A Listen and write a ✓.

	 🐄	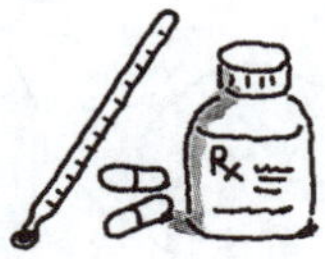 💊	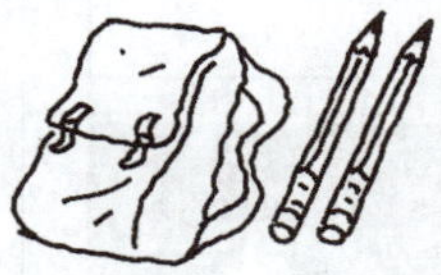 🎒	 📋
1. Miss Smith 		✓		
2. Mr. and Mrs. Long 				
3. Ben 				
4. Mr. and Mrs. Jones 				

B Listen and fill in the blanks.

| students | a taxi driver | a cook | shopkeepers |

1.  He's __a cook__.

2.  She's _____.

3.  They're _____.

4.  They're _____.

23

Review Unit

A Look and write.

1. a teacher
2.
3.
4.
5.
6.

B Read and match.

1. Who is he?   •   • They are Mr. and Mrs. Hill. They are cooks.

2. What are these?   •   • It is a car.

3. Who are they?   •   • She is Miss Bates.

4. What is that?   •   • He is Ben.

5. Who is she?   •   • They are puzzles.

24

A. Unscramble the questions and answer them.

1. these / balls / Are

   Are these balls ?

   No, they are not.

2. she / shopkeeper / Is / a

   _____ ?

   _____ .

3. a / Is / that / yo-yo

   _____ ?

   _____ .

4. Are / police / they / officers

   _____ ?

   _____ .

B. Listen and circle.

1. a. That's too bad.
   b. I'm sick. *(circled)*

2. a. How are you?
   b. See you later.

3. a. She's Sally.
   b. They're Ben and Sally.

4. a. Yes, it is.
   b. Yes, they are.

Unit 3

A. Fill in the blanks.

16 North Street   Hillsdale   798-2043

Where do you live, Jenny?

I live in ___Hillsdale.___

What's your address?

It's _____

What's your telephone number?

It's _____

B. Read and write.

What about you?

1. Where do you live?

   I live in _____

2. What's your address?

3. What's your telephone number?

Look, read, and write.

1. Joe Smith
   14 Main Street
   Hillsdale
   359-4716

2. Mary Young
   19 Brown Street
   Hillsdale
   815-8115

3. Peter Jones
   10 Hill Street
   Hillsdale
   934-6542

1. Name   Joe Smith
   Address   14 Main Street
                    Hillsdale
   Telephone Number 359-4716

2. Name
   Address

   Telephone Number

3. Name
   Address

   Telephone Number

Look, read, and number.

1. house
2. bathroom
3. living room
4. bedroom
5. kitchen
6. dining room
7. TV
8. sink
9. bed
10. refrigerator
11. sofa
12. toilet
13. stove
14. lamp
15. bathtub

A. Match, read, and write.

| 1. | 2. | 3. | 4. |

bathroom — living room — bedroom — kitchen

1. Where is the sofa?

It's in the living room.

2. Where is the stove?

3. Where is the toilet?

4. Where is the bed?

B. Look, read, and write.

1. Is the TV in the bathroom?

No, it is not.

2. Is the table in the dining room?

3. Is the bathtub in the kitchen?

29

A. Read and circle.

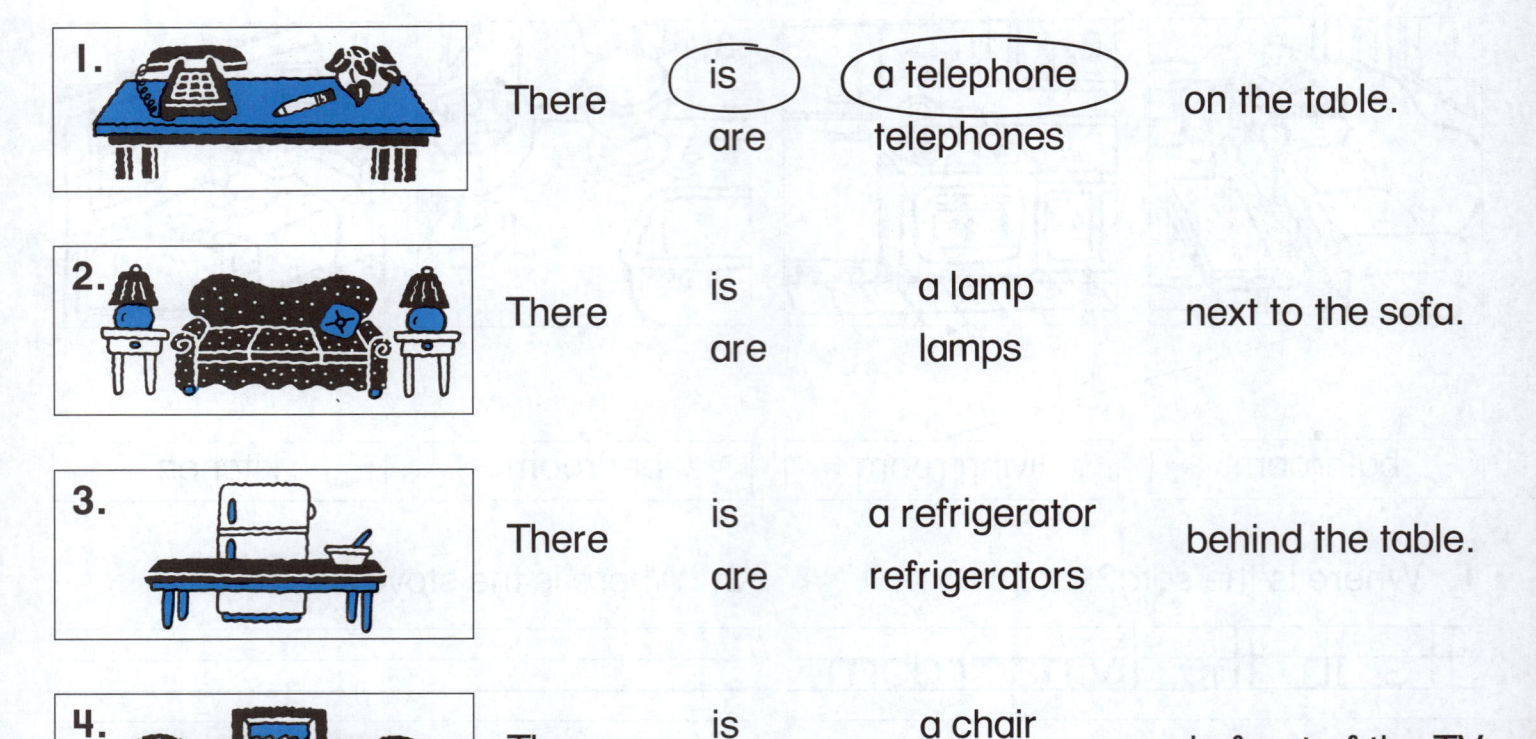

1. There (is) / are (a telephone) / telephones on the table.

2. There is / are a lamp / lamps next to the sofa.

3. There is / are a refrigerator / refrigerators behind the table.

4. There is / are a chair / chairs in front of the TV.

B. Change the sentences.

1. There is a lamp next to the sofa.

There are lamps next to the sofa.

2. There is a bed in the bedroom.

3. There is a table behind the sofa.

30

A. Look and write.

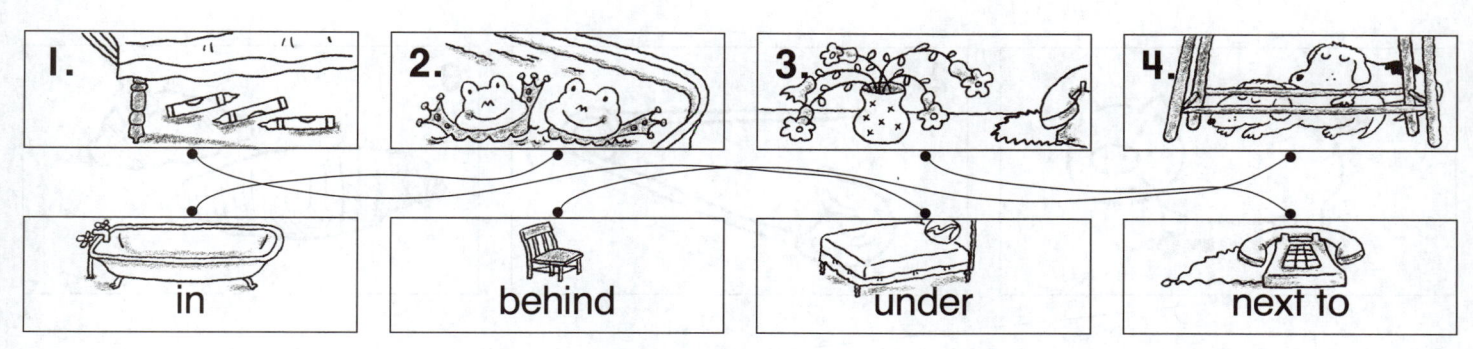

1. There are crayons under the bed.
2.
3.
4.

B. Answer the questions.

1. Is there a table in front of the sofa?
   Yes, there is.

2. Are there books on the desk?

3. Is there a cat under the chair?

A. Listen and match.

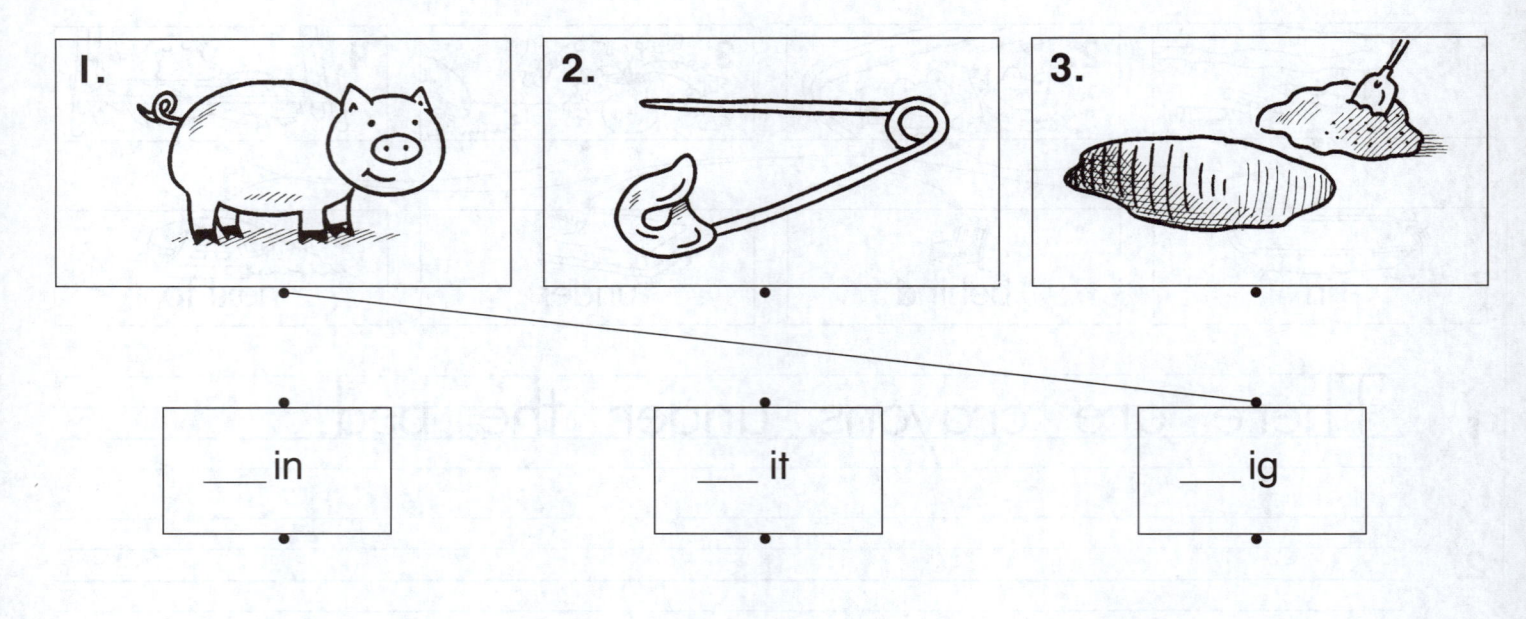

1. ___in
2. ___it
3. ___ig

4. 
5. 
6.

B. Listen and write a ✓ or an ✗.

1. ✗
2. 
3.
4.

32

A Listen and match.

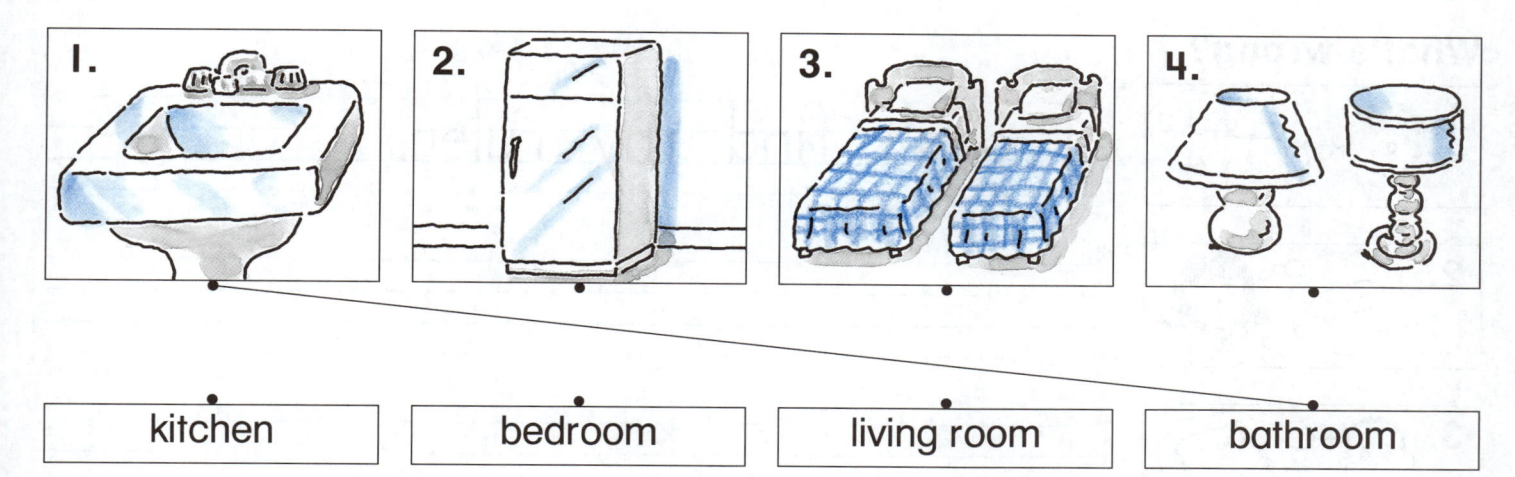

| 1. | 2. | 3. | 4. |

kitchen | bedroom | living room | bathroom

B Listen and draw.

1. 2. 3.

C Listen and write.

1. 2. 3.

464-9392

33

Unit 4

A Look and write.

What's wrong?

1. I can't find my ruler.
2.
3.
4.

B Unscramble the sentences.

1. wrong/What's/?

   What's wrong?

2. book/can't/my/I/find/.

3. your/it/bedroom/Is/in/?

4. don't/I/know/.

A Look, read, and match.

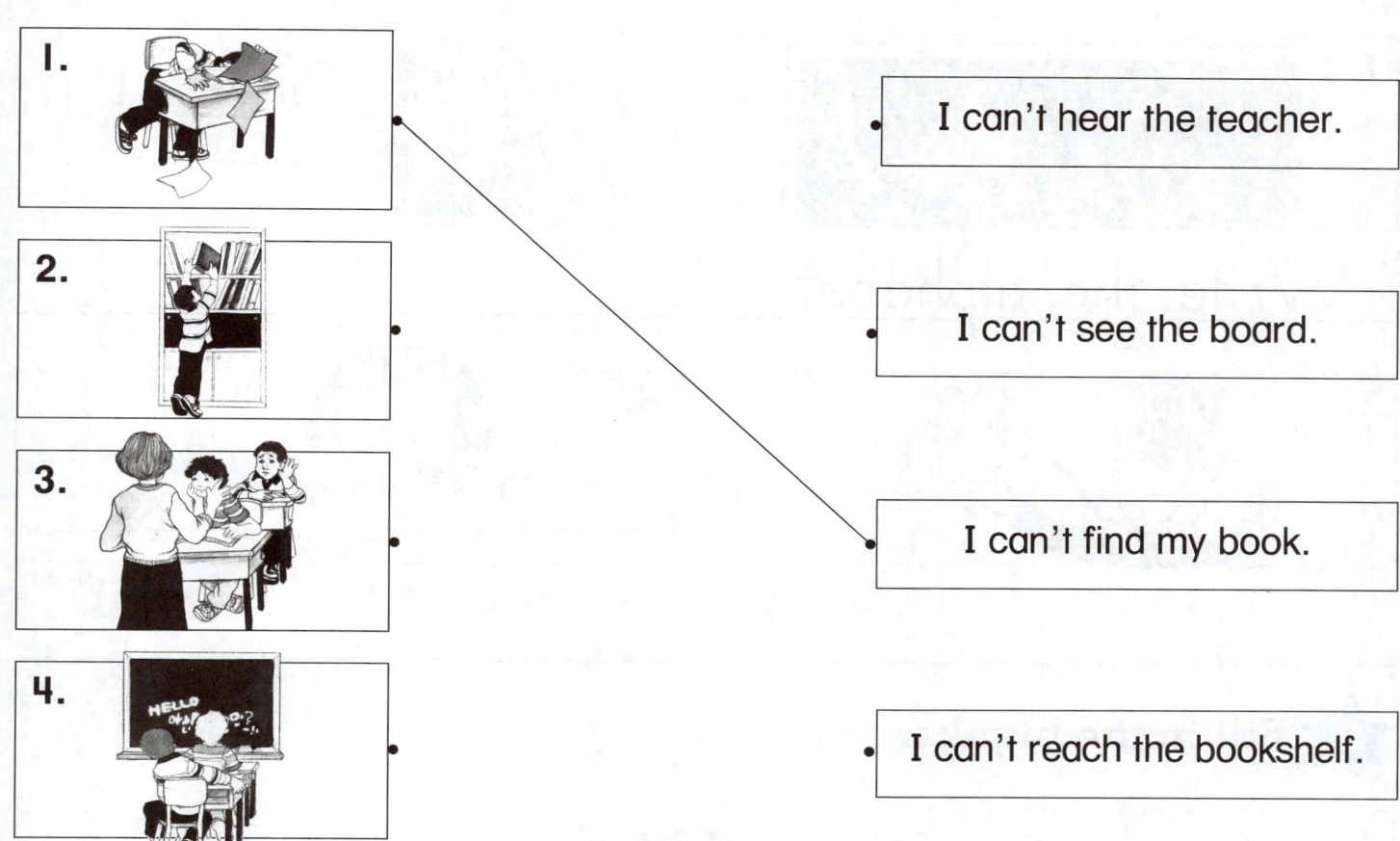

1. • — • I can't hear the teacher.

2. • — • I can't see the board.

3. • — • I can't find my book.

4. • — • I can't reach the bookshelf.

B Choose the correct answer.

__b__ 1. I can't find my ___pencil___.
   a. board   b. pencil   c. bookshelf

_____ 2. I can't hear the _____.
   a. teacher   b. pencil   c. board

_____ 3. I can't reach the _____.
   a. teacher   b. board   c. bookshelf

_____ 4. I can't see the _____.
   a. pencil   b. board   c. book

35

A. Look and write.

1. Write the alphabet.

2.

3.

4.

B. Fill in the blanks.

1. Look at me !
   I can sing a song .

2. Look at _____!
   He can _____.

3. Look at _____!
   She can _____.

4. Look at _____!
   I can _____.

A Look and write.

1. climb a tree
2. swim
3. ride a bike
4. write his name

What can he/she do?

1. She can climb a tree.
2.
3.
4.

B Make questions.

1. What can he do?

   He can play with a yo-yo.

2.

   She can draw a picture.

3.

   He can jump rope.

4.

   She can play baseball.

A. Read and write.

1. She can ride a bicycle. + She can't fly a kite. =
   She can ride a bicycle, but she can't fly a kite.

2. He can swim. + He can't play baseball. =
   _____

3. She can jump rope. + She can't climb a tree. =
   _____

4. He can speak English. + He can't write the alphabet. =
   _____

B. Look and write.

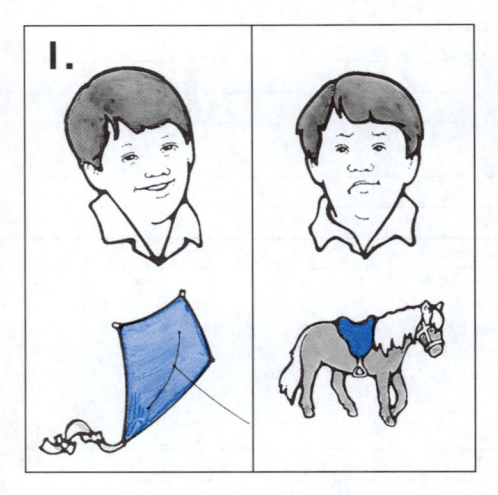

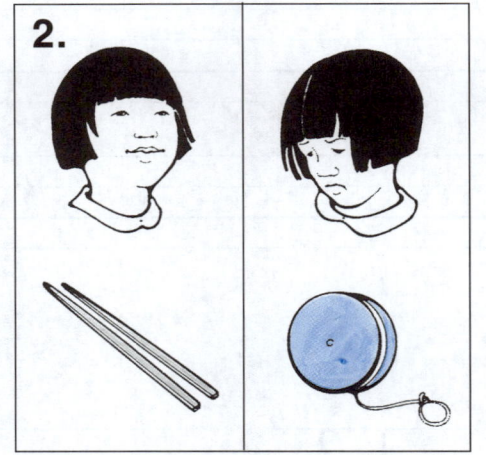

1. He can fly a kite, but he can't ride a pony.
2. _____
3. _____

A. Look and write.

1. Can he ride a pony?
No, he can't.

2. Can she fly a kite?

3. Can he do a magic trick?

4. Can she write the alphabet?

B. Read and write a ✓.

Can you _____ ?	How are You? / Fine, thank You!			
Yes	✓			
No				

A Listen and choose the word with the different sound.

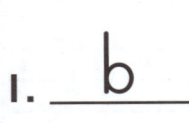

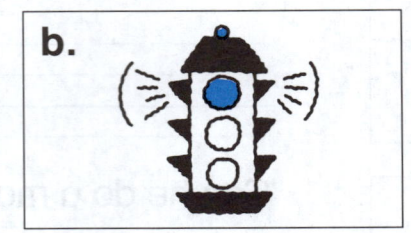

1. __b__   a. (dog)   b. (mop)   c. (log)
2. _____   a. (top)   b. (stop) c. (run)
3. _____   a. (fun)   b. (frog) c. (sun)

B Listen and write *og*, *op*, or *un*.

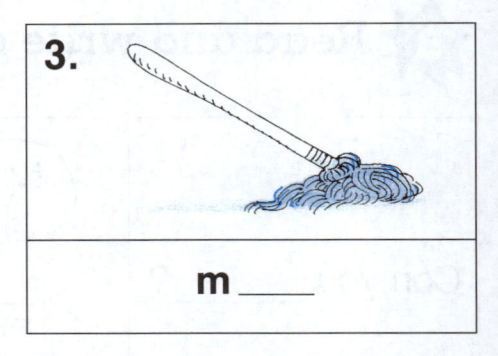

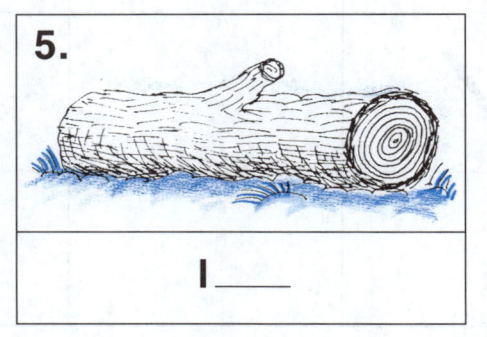

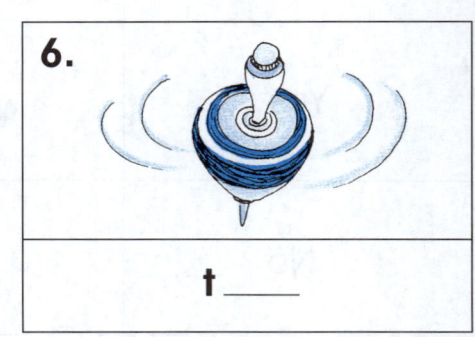

1. fr__og__
2. r____
3. m____
4. f____
5. l____
6. t____

40

A. Listen and match.

1.
2.
3.
4.

B. Listen and complete the sentences.

1. She can dance, — but she can't sing a song.
2. He can ride a bicycle, — but he can't draw a picture.
3. She can fly a kite,
4. He can play baseball,

- but he can't ride a pony.
- but she can't climb a tree.

C. Listen and write a ✓ or an ✗.

1. ✗
2.
3.
4.

41

Review Unit

A. Look for the words.

a	f	t	e	l	e	p	h	o	n	e	a
c	e	o	d	a	g	m	t	u	v	b	l
h	s	i	c	m	k	q	b	e	d	i	k
a	o	l	b	p	l	s	t	o	v	e	a
i	f	e	h	j	o	r	s	w	x	z	t
r	a	t	i	n	b	a	t	h	t	u	b
r	e	f	r	i	g	e	r	a	t	o	r

chair, lamp, toilet, stove, sofa,  bed,  refrigerator,  telephone, bathtub

B. Look, read, and write.

1. __c__ There is a lamp __behind__ the sofa.
   a. in front of   b. next to   c. behind

2. _____ There is a sink _____ the refrigerator.
   a. next to   b. in front of   c. behind

3. _____ There are balls _____ the bed.
   a. on   b. under   c. by

A **Read and match.**

1. What can you do? • • No, there aren't.

2. Where is the stove? • • I can dance.

3. Can he swim? • • Yes, I can.

4. Are there beds in the kitchen? • • It's in the kitchen.

5. Can you use chopsticks? • • No, he can't.

B **Listen and circle.**

1. (a. I can't find my book.) 2. a. Thanks, Mom!
   b. I can't see the board.   b. I don't know.

3. a. It's 798-2043. 4. a. I live in Hillsdale.
   b. It's 789-0234.   b. It's 16 North Street.

Unit 5

A Read, arrange, and write.

a. I do, too.
b. Yes, please.
c. What's for lunch?
d. Do you want spaghetti?
e. Mmm. That's good. I like spaghetti.
f. Spaghetti.

1. __C__   2. _____
3. _____   4. _____
5. _____   6. _____

B Look and write.

1. Do you want chicken?
No, thank you.

2. Do you want fish?

3. Do you want spaghetti?

4. Do you want pizza?

A Read and write.

1. Do you like __spaghetti__?
   Yes, __I do.__
   I __do__, too.

2. Do you like _____?

3. Do you like _____?

B Look, match, and write.

Do you like _____?

| 1. chicken | 2. ice cream | 3. fish |

_____   Yes, I do.   _____

45

A. Look and write.

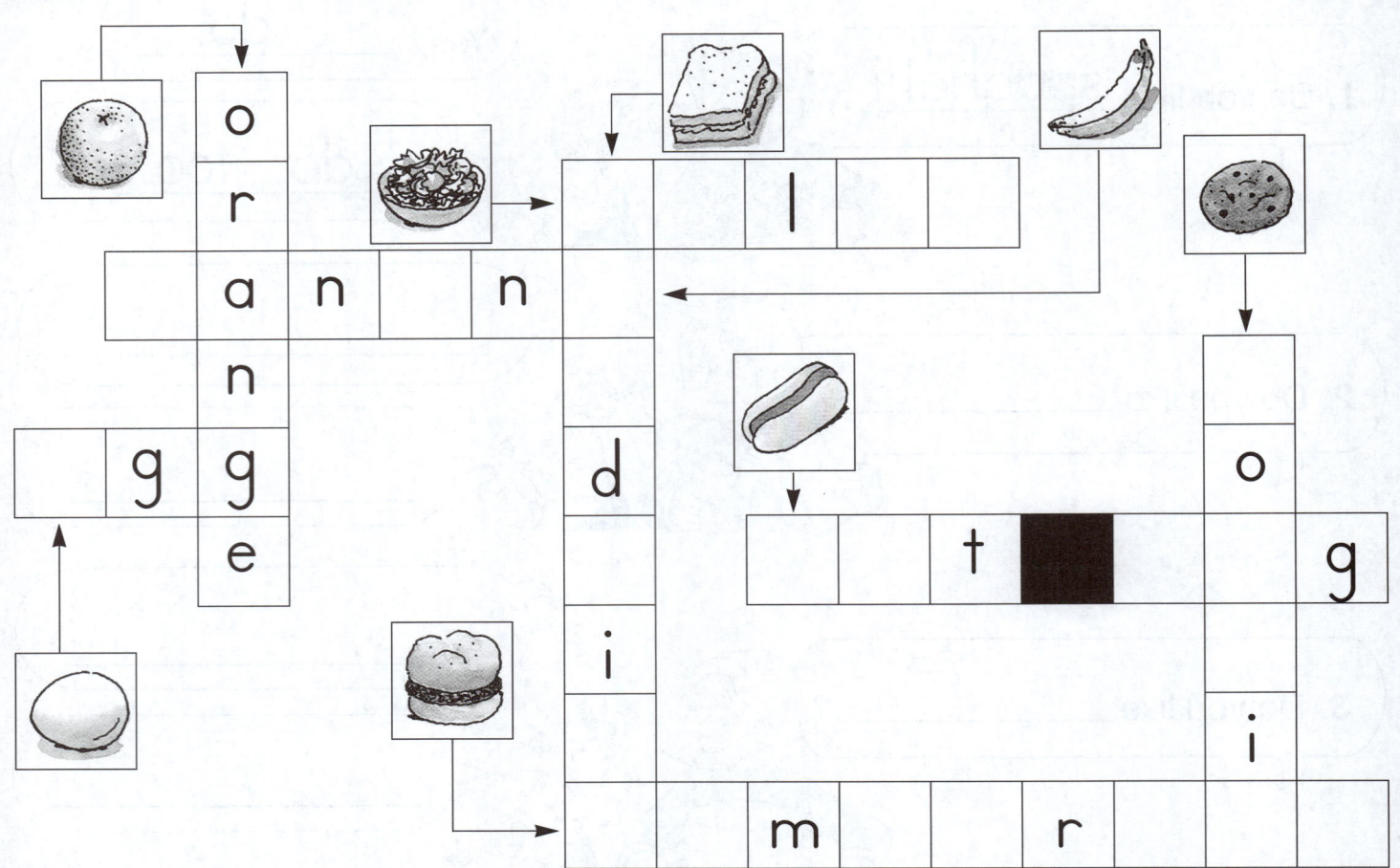

(crossword puzzle with food words)

B. Read and write.

1. What do you want?
I want a hot dog.
What about Roy? What does he want?
He wants a hot dog, too.

2. What do you want?

What about Julie? What does she want?

A. Answer the questions.

1. Does he want an egg?
   No, he doesn't.

2. Does she want a hamburger?

3. Does he want a salad?

B. Make questions and fill in the blanks.

1. Does she want a cookie ?   Yes, she does.

2. _____ ?   No, he _____.

3. _____ ?   Yes, she _____.

4. _____ ?   No, he _____.

47

A Look and write.

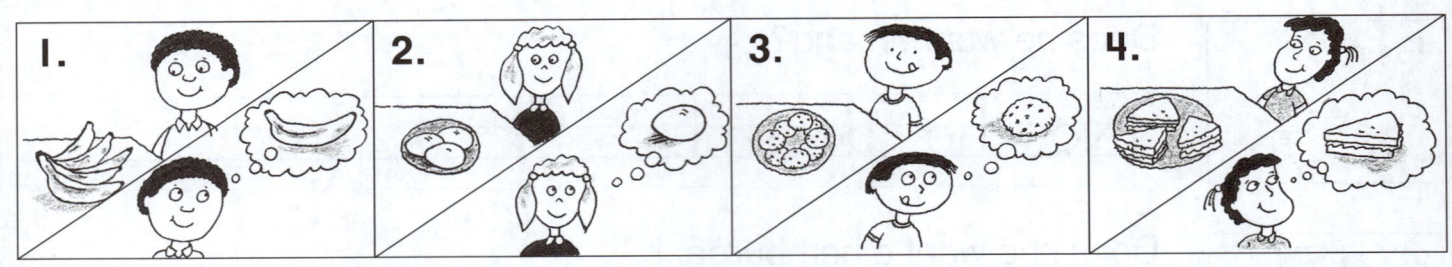

1. He likes <u>bananas</u>.

   He wants <u>a</u> <u>banana</u>.

2. She likes _____.

   She wants _____ _____.

3. He _____ _____.

   He _____ ____ _____.

4. ____ _____ _____.
   ____ ____ _____.

B Look, read, and match.

| What does Amy like? | What does Roy like? | What does Julie like? |

| She likes salads. | She likes oranges. | He likes hamburgers. |

48

A Look, read, and write.

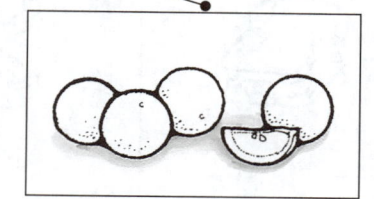

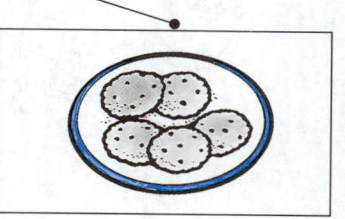

1. Does he like oranges?

No, he doesn't.

3. Does he like cookies?

2. Does she like eggs?

4. Does she like hamburgers?

B Unscramble and match.

1. he / bananas / Does / like / ?

Does he like bananas?

2. hot dogs / Does / like / she / ?

3. like / he / Does / salads / ?

No, she doesn't.

Yes, he does.

Yes, he does.

49

A. Listen and fill in the blanks with *ame*, *ake*, or *ay*.

1. cr<u>ay</u>on
2. n___
3. sn___
4. m___
5. s___
6. pl___
7. g___
8. c___
9. gr___

B. Listen and write.

1. Pl <u>a y</u> with a cr __ __ on.

2. Can you n __ __ __ the g __ __ __ ?

3. Can a sn __ __ __ m __ __ __ a c __ __ __ ?

A Listen and circle.

1. He wants a hamburger.
      (likes hamburgers.)

2. She wants a salad.
       likes salads.

3. He wants a banana.
      likes bananas.

4. She wants a cookie.
       likes cookies.

B Listen and write a ✓ or an ✗.

1. ✗ / ✓

2.

3.

4.

51

Unit 6

A. Read and match.

1. Whose watch is that? — No, her watch is blue.
2. Is it Jenny's watch? — I don't know.
3. Is it John's watch? — I know! It's Andy's watch.
4. Whose watch is it? — No, his watch is green.

B. Unscramble the sentences.

1. watch / it / Whose / is / ?

   Whose watch is it?

2. her / blue / No, / is / watch / .

3. John's / Is / watch / it / ?

52

A. Look, read, and write.

1. Whose hat is that? It's Andy's hat.

2. Whose books are those?

3. Whose cat is that?

B. Change the sentences.

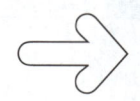

1. Whose hat is that? ⇒ Whose hats are those?

2. It's Kate's book. ⇒

3. Whose cat is this? ⇒

4. This is Andy's pen. ⇒

5. That's John's pencil. ⇒

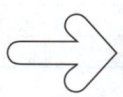

53

A Look and choose.

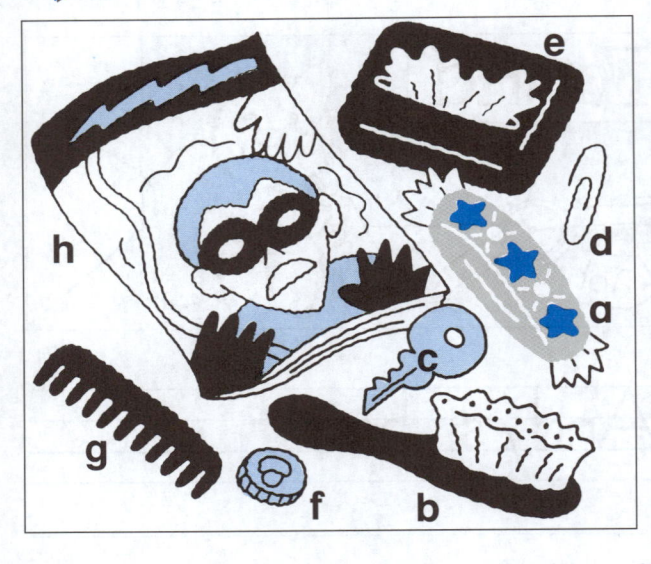

1. _b_ a brush 2. ____ a comic book
3. ____ a key 4. ____ a coin
5. ____ a tissue 6. ____ a comb
7. ____ a paper clip 8. ____ a candy bar

B Look, read, and write.

What do you have in your bag?

1. I have a brush.

2. ____

3. ____

4. ____

54

A. Look, read, and write.

1. Do you have a pencil in your bag?
No, I don't.

2. Do you have a candy bar in your bag?

3. Do you have a key in your bag?

B. Look and write.

1. Do you have a tissue in your bag?
No, I don't.

2. _____?
Yes, __ ___.

3. _____?
No, __ _____.

A Look and write.

1. She has a yo-yo in her hand.
2.
3.
4.

B Circle and fill in the blanks.

1. What does (he)/she have in (his)/her hand?
   (He)/She has a ___ruler___.

2. What does he/she have in his/her hand?
   He/She has a _____.

3. What does he/she have in his/her hand?
   He/She has a _____.

A. Write the words.

1. a notebook
2. _____
3. _____
4. _____
5. _____

1. _____
2. _____
3. _____
4. _____
5. _____

B. Answer the questions.

1. Does he have a key in his bag?

Yes, he does.

2. Does he have a tissue?

3. Does he have a paper clip?

4. Does she have a comb in her bag?

5. Does she have a cassette?

6. Does she have a pencil case?

A Listen and write a ✓ or an ✗.

1. -ea-	a. ✓	b.	c.	d.
2. -ee-	a.	b.	c.	d.
3. -e	a.	b.	c.	d.

B Listen and match.

1. (tree)
2. (girl)
3. (reading)

read
ice cream

tree
sleep

she
he

4. (boy)
5. (ice cream)
6. (sleeping)

58

A Listen and match.

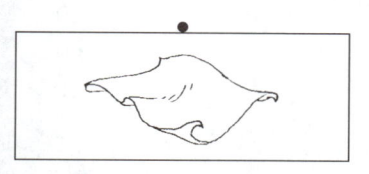

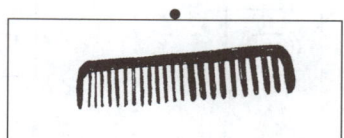

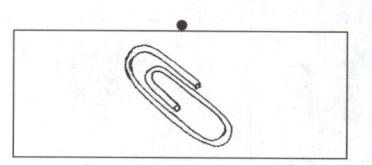

1. 2. 3. 4.

B Listen and draw.

1. 2. 3.

C Listen and write a ✓ or an ✗.

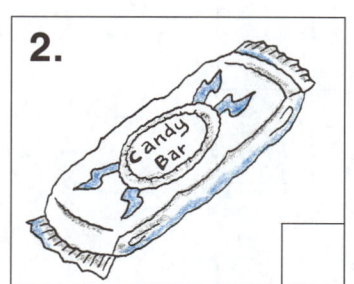

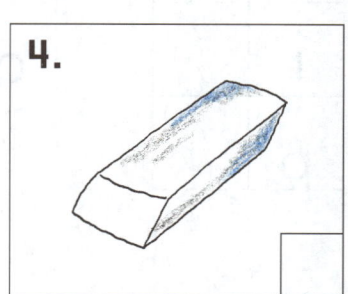

1. ✗ 2. 3. 4.

What about you?

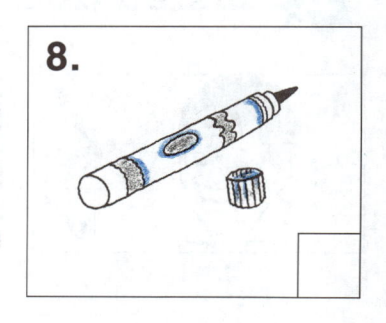

5. 6. 7. 8.

59

Review Unit

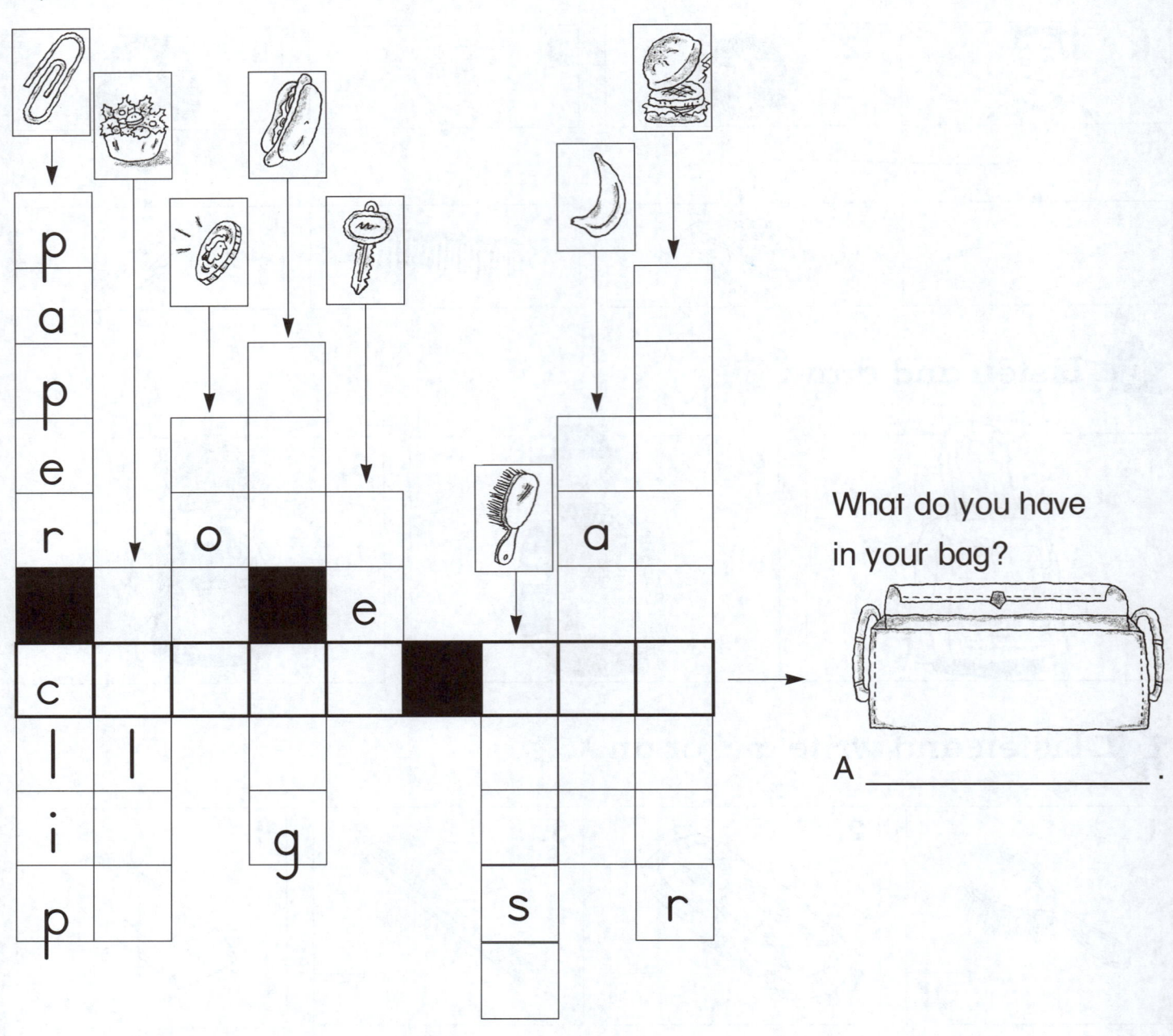

A Look and write.

p
a
p
e
r
c
l
i
p

o
e
g

a
s

r

What do you have in your bag?

A _____.

B Listen and write a ✓ or an ✗.

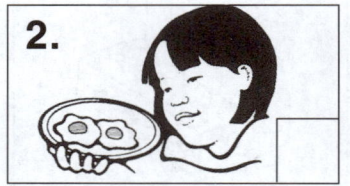

1. ✓
2.
3.
4.

60

A Read and choose.

__b__ 1. Do you want spaghetti?
   a. I do, too.
   b. Yes, please.

___ 2. Whose watch is that?
   a. I don't know.
   b. No, her watch is blue.

___ 3. What's for lunch?
   a. That's good.
   b. Spaghetti.

___ 4. Is it John's watch?
   a. I know. It's Andy's watch.
   b. No, his watch is green.

B Listen and draw.

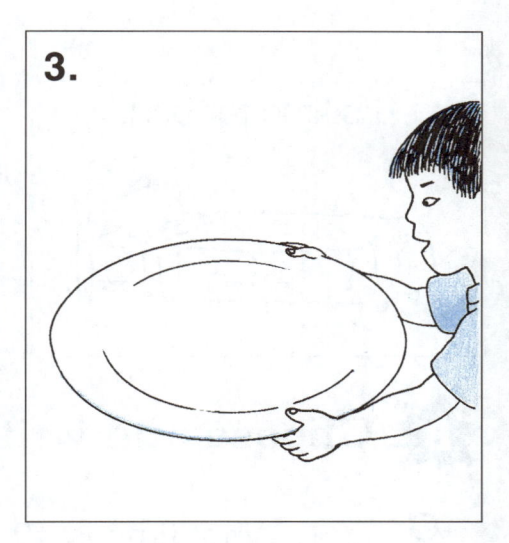

Unit 7

A. Read and match.

1. What time is it? 
2. What time is it? 
3. What time is it?

It's seven o'clock.   It's eight o'clock.   It's six o'clock.

It's time for bed.   It's time for dinner.    It's time for your bath.

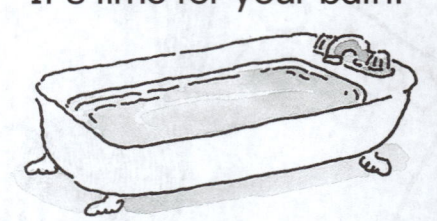

B. Choose and write.

__a__ 1. What time is it?
   a. It's six o'clock.
   b. Yes, it is.

_____ 2. Is it time for bed?
   a. Yes, it is.
   b. It's eight o'clock.

_____ 3. It's time for your bath, Scott.
   a. Good night, Mom.
   b. OK.

62

A. Read and draw.

1. It's six o'clock.
2. It's eight o'clock.
3. It's nine o'clock.
4. It's twelve o'clock.

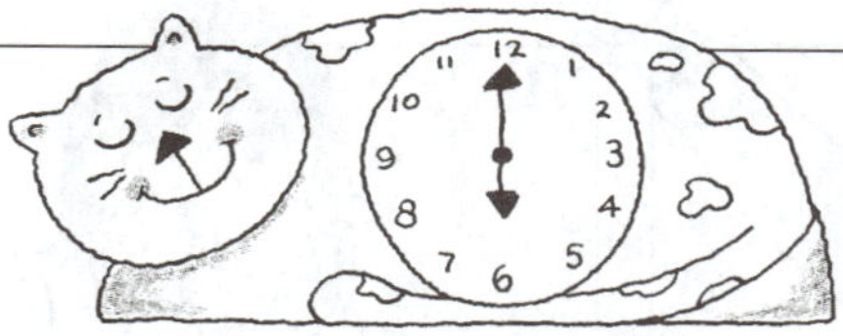

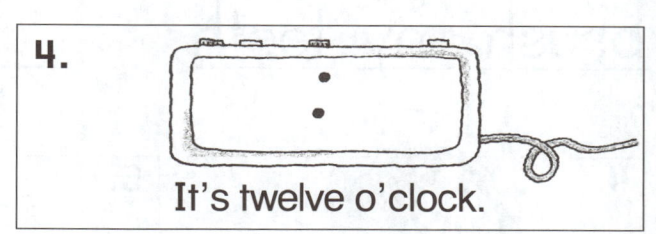

B. Fill in the blanks.

| twelve | six | eight | nine |
| lunch | dinner | school | bed |

1. It's __eight__ o'clock.
   It's time for __school__.

2. It's _____ o'clock.
   It's time for _____.

3. It's _____ o'clock.
   It's time for _____.

4. It's _____ o'clock.
   It's time for _____.

A Look and write.

1. brush my teeth
2. _____
3. _____
4. _____
5. _____
6. _____

B Look, read, and write.

What do you do in the morning?

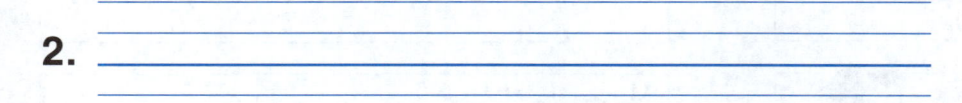

1. I get up.
2. _____
3. _____
4. _____

64

Look at the pictures and answer the questions.

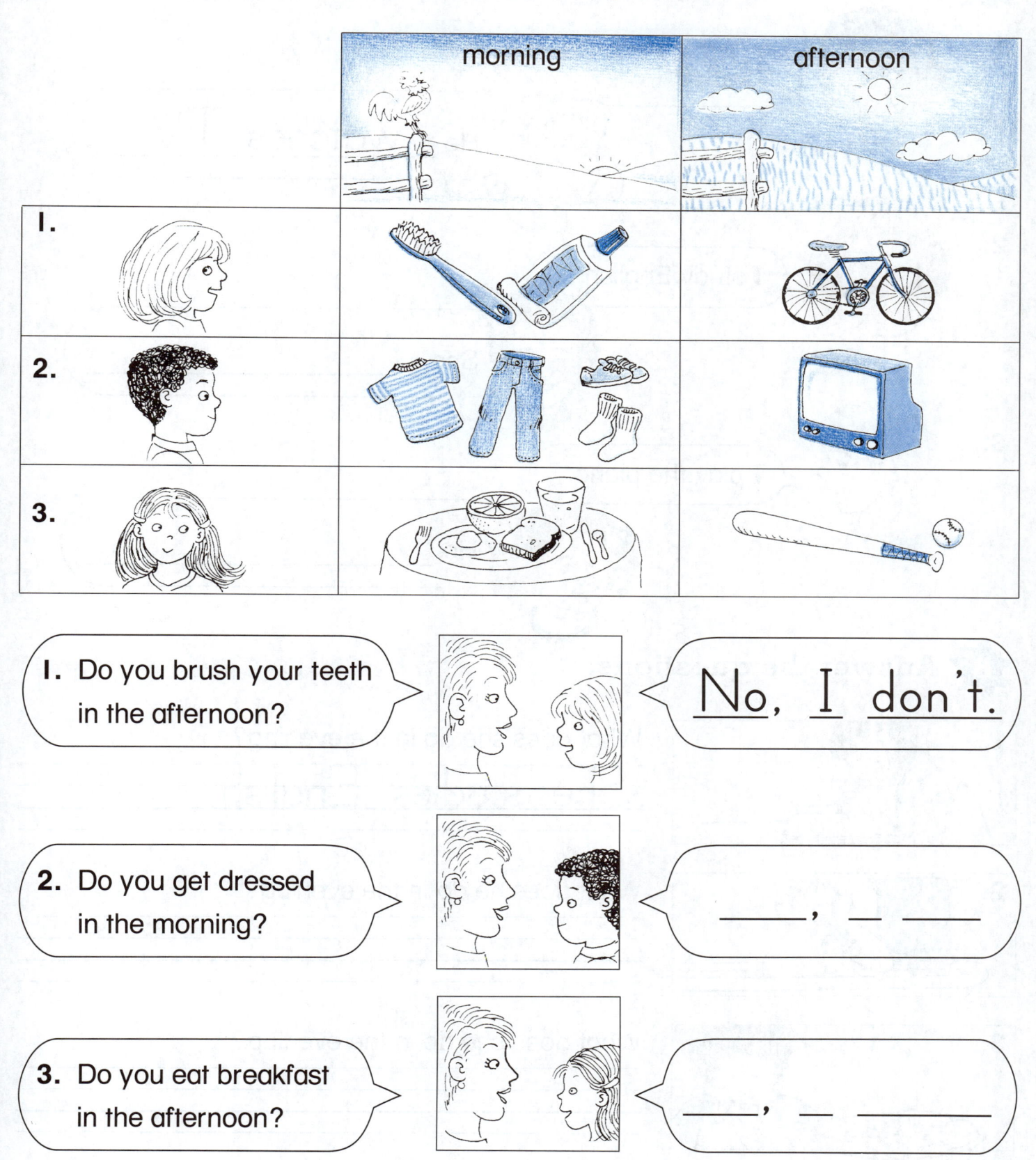

1. Do you brush your teeth in the afternoon? — No, I don't.

2. Do you get dressed in the morning? — ___, __ ___

3. Do you eat breakfast in the afternoon? — ___, __ ___

65

A Read and write.

1. I watch TV.
   He <u>watches TV.</u>

2. I study English.
   She _____

3.  I play the piano.
   He _____

B Answer the questions.

1.  What does she do in the evening?
   She studies English.

2.  What does he do in the evening?
   _____

3.  What does she do in the evening?
   _____

A Look and write.

1. morning
2. _____
3. _____
4. _____

B Fill in the blanks and answer the questions.

| eat breakfast | get dressed | go to bed | climb a tree |

1. Does he ___get dressed___ in the evening?
   No, ___he doesn't___.

2. Does she _____ at night?
   Yes, _____.

3. Does he _____ in the afternoon?
   No, _____.

4. Does she _____ in the morning?
   Yes, _____.

67

A. Listen and write a ✓ or an X.

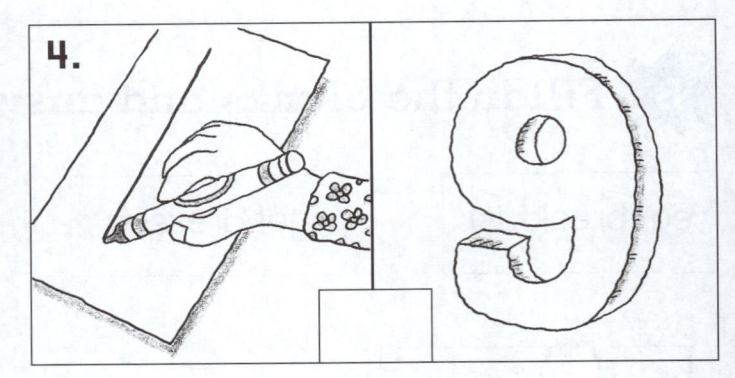

1. [tree] | [kite] ✗
2. [mice] | [ice block]
3. [rice bowl] | [hand writing]
4. [hand with crayon] | [9]

B. Listen and circle the letters.

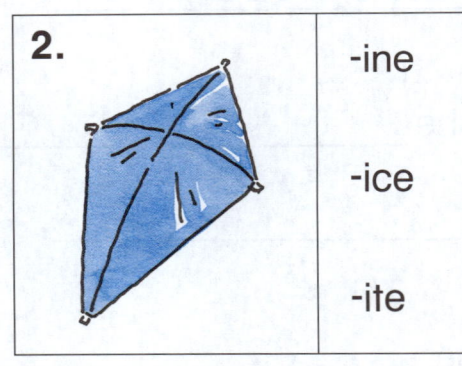

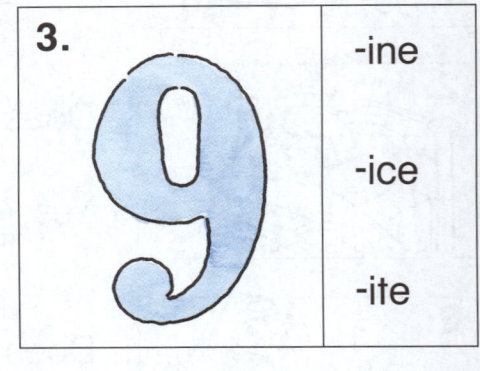

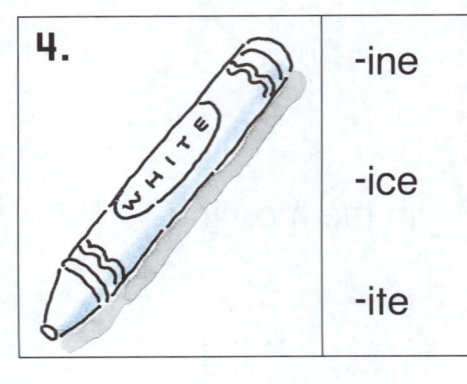

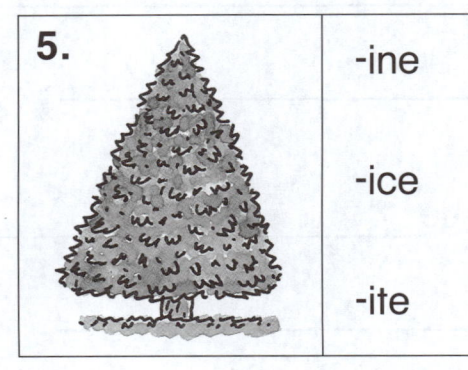

1. [rice bowl] — -ine / (-ice) / -ite
2. [kite] — -ine / -ice / -ite
3. [9] — -ine / -ice / -ite
4. [white crayon] — -ine / -ice / -ite
5. [pine tree] — -ine / -ice / -ite
6. [mice] — -ine / -ice / -ite

68

A. Listen and match.

1. 2. 3. 4.

in the morning  | in the afternoon  | in the evening  | at night

B. Listen and write the number.

He watches TV.	He gets up.	He takes a bath.	He studies English.
	1		

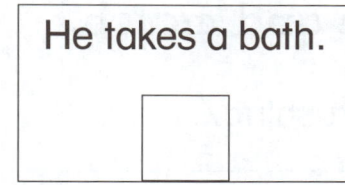

C. Listen and choose.

__b__ 1. a. Yes, he does. b. Yes, she does.

____ 2. a. No, she doesn't. b. No, he doesn't.

____ 3. a. Yes, he does. b. Yes, I do.

____ 4. a. No, I don't. b. No, she doesn't.

Unit 8

A Look and write.

1. What are you doing?

I'm washing my face.

2. What are you doing?

_____

B Unscramble and match.

1. teeth / I'm / my / brushing / .

I'm brushing my teeth.

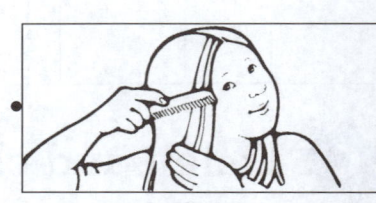

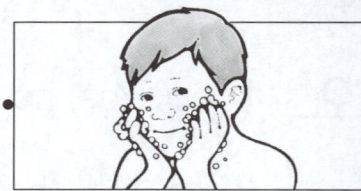

2. combing / hair / my / I'm / .

_____

3. my / face / I'm / washing / .

_____

A Look and write.

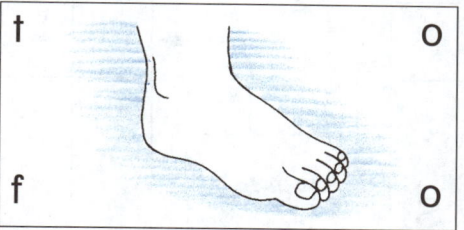

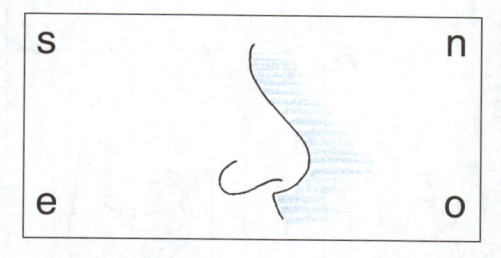

e　　　　d	t　　　　o	s　　　　n
h　　　　a	f　　　　o	e　　　　o

1. ___head___　　2. _____　　3. _____

k　　　　e	c　　　　k	n　　　　d
e　　　　n	n　　　　e	a　　　　h

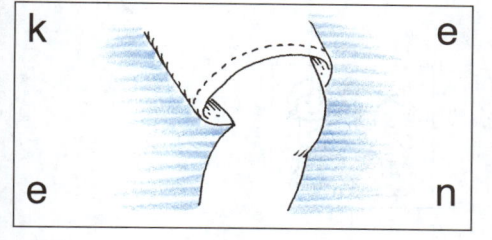

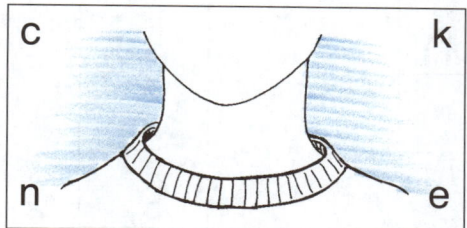

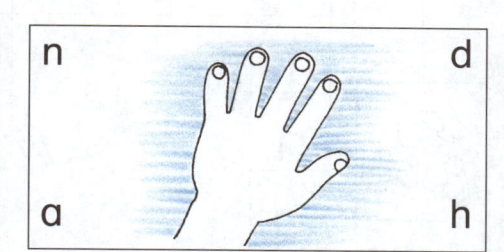

4. _____　　5. _____　　6. _____

B Read and draw.

1. ear 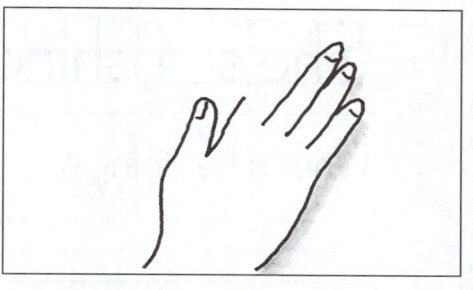　　2. finger 　　3. mouth

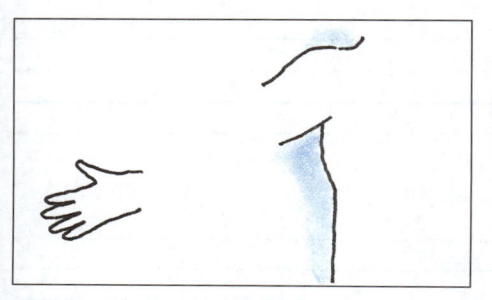

4. arm 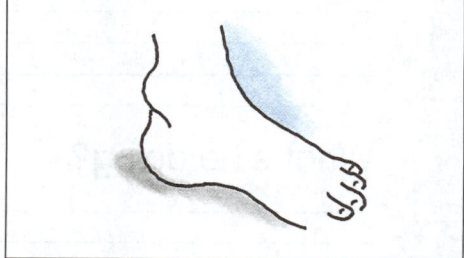　　5. toe 　　6. eye

A Look and write.

1. coloring / running / singing / fishing

2. sleeping / swimming / playing

B Read and write.

1. What's she doing?
   She's fishing.

2. What's he doing?

3. What's she doing?

4. What's he doing?

72

A. Look, read, and write.

1. Is she coloring?   No, she isn't.

2. Is he swimming?

3. Is she running?

4. Is he sleeping?

B. Look, read, and write.

1. playing   Is she playing?
   No, she isn't.

2. fishing

3. sleeping

A Read and write.

1. She is at home. ⇒ She's at home.

2. Where is John? ⇒

3. He is watching TV. ⇒

B Look, read, and write.

Ted	Jean	Sue	Mr. Lee
buying juice	sleeping	flying a kite	reading a book

1. Where's Mr. Lee?   He's at school.
   What's he doing?   He's reading a book.

2. Where's Ted?
   What's he doing?

3. Where's Sue?
   What's she doing?

4. Where's Jean?
   What's she doing?

74

A Look, read, and match.

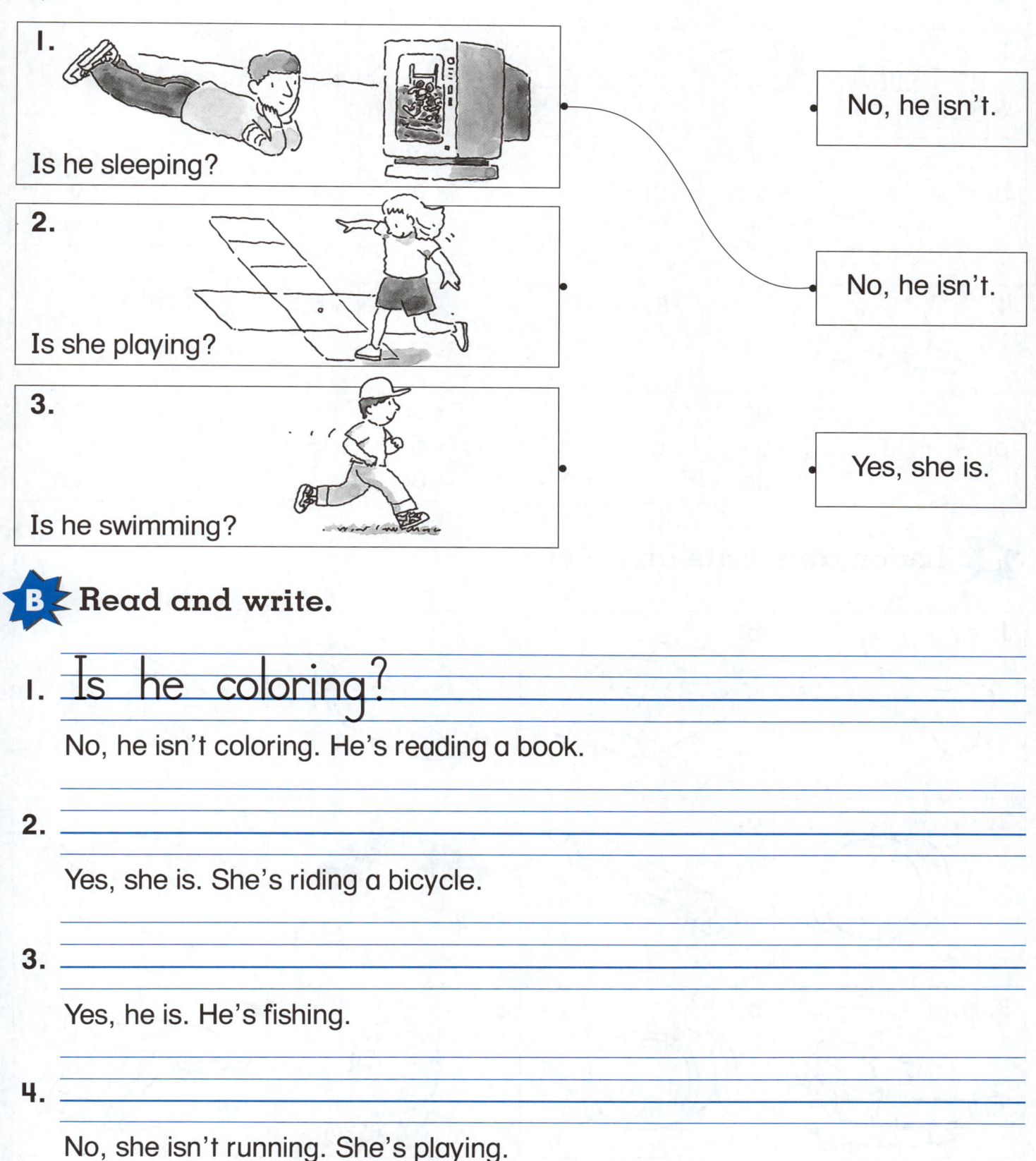

1. Is he sleeping?
2. Is she playing?
3. Is he swimming?

No, he isn't.
No, he isn't.
Yes, she is.

B Read and write.

1. Is he coloring?

   No, he isn't coloring. He's reading a book.

2. _____

   Yes, she is. She's riding a bicycle.

3. _____

   Yes, he is. He's fishing.

4. _____

   No, she isn't running. She's playing.

A. Listen and match. 🎧

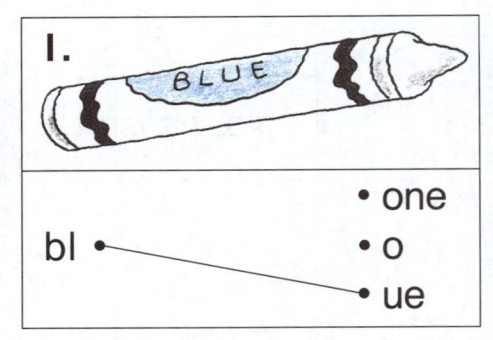

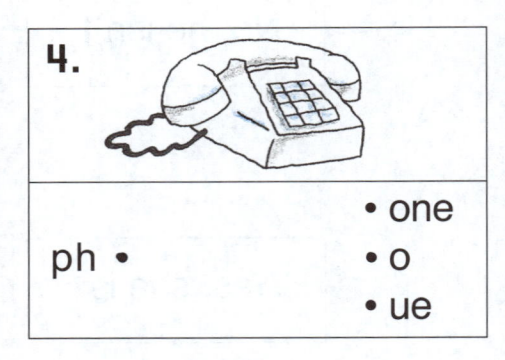

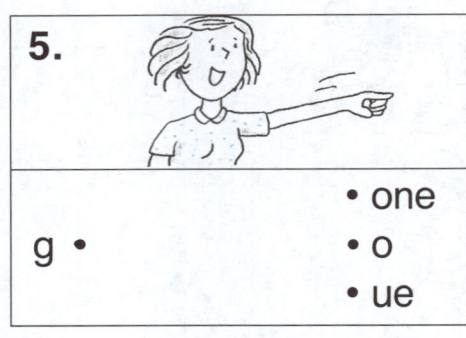

1. bl • — • ue   • one • o
2. st •   • one • o • ue
3. n •   • one • o • ue
4. ph •   • one • o • ue
5. g •   • one • o • ue
6. S •   • one • o • ue

B. Listen and write an X. 🎧

1. a.   b.   c.   d.
2. a.   b.   c.   d.
3. a.   b.   c.   d.

76

A Listen and write a ✓.

	fishing	coloring	running	swimming	playing
1.			✓		
2.					
3.					
4.					
5.					

B Listen and circle.

1.
   a. He's at home.
   b. He's at school. *(circled)*

2.
   a. No, he isn't.
   b. Yes, he is.

3.
   a. She's at the park.
   b. She's at the store.

4.
   a. She's flying a kite.
   b. She's playing.

5.
   a. Yes, he is.
   b. No, he isn't.

6.
   a. He's sleeping.
   b. He's watching TV.

77

Review Unit

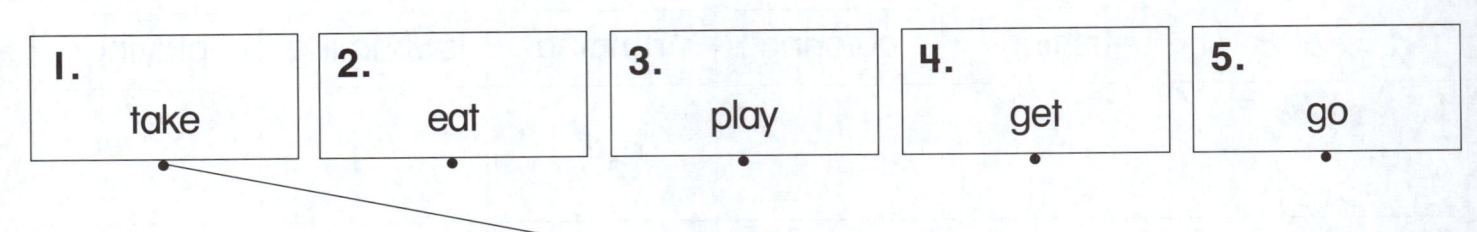

A Read and match.

| 1. take | 2. eat | 3. play | 4. get | 5. go |

| the piano | dressed | a bath | to bed | breakfast |

B Read and choose.

__a__ 1. What do you do in the morning?
  a. I brush my teeth.
  b. I go to bed.

_____ 2. What do you do in the afternoon?
  a. I do homework.
  b. I get dressed.

_____ 3. What do you do in the evening?
  a. I eat breakfast.
  b. I watch TV.

_____ 4. What do you do at night?
  a. I take a bath.
  b. I eat dinner.

A Read and match.

1. What time is it? — It's six o'clock.
2. Hello, Mrs. Hill. Where's Kate? — She's at the park.
3. What are you doing? — I'm washing my face.
4. Is it time for bed?   — Yes, it is.

B Listen and circle.

1.
   a. She's combing her hair.
   b. She combs her hair. ⟵ (circled)

2.
   a. Yes, he is.
   b. Yes, he does.

3.
   a. I'm coloring.
   b. I color.

4.
   a. No, she doesn't.
   b. No, she isn't.